The Dairy-Free Kitchen

Quarto is the authority on a wide range of topics.

Quarto educates, entertains and enriches the lives of
our readers—enthusiasts and lovers of hands-on living.

www.QuartoKnows.com

© 2014 Fair Winds Press
Text © 2014 Ashley Adams
Photography © 2014 Fair Winds Press

First published in the USA in 2014 by
Fair Winds Press, an imprint of
Quarto Publishing Group USA Inc.
100 Cummings Center
Suite 406-L
Beverly, MA 01915-6101
Telephone: (978) 282-9590
Fax: (978) 283-2742
QuartoKnows.com
Visit our blogs at QuartoKnows.com

ISBN: 978-1-59233-573-2

Digital edition published in 2014
eISBN: 978-1-61058-873-7

Library of Congress Cataloging-in-Publication Data

Adams, Ashley, 1984-
The dairy-free kitchen : 100 recipes for all the creamy foods you love—without lactose,
casein, or dairy / Ashley Adams.
    pages cm
Includes bibliographical references and index.
ISBN 978-1-59233-573-2 (paperback)—ISBN 978-1-61058-873-7 (digital edition)
1. Milk-free diet—Recipes. 2. Milk-free diet. I. Title.
RM234.5.A33 2013
 641.3'02--dc23
                                     2013024832

Cover and book design by Carol Holtz | holtzdesign.com
Photography by Ashley and Brian Adams
Image on page 21 by Adam Gault | Getty Images

Printed and bound in USA

The information in this book is for educational purposes only. It is not intended
to replace the advice of a physician or medical practitioner. Please see your
health care provider before beginning any new health program.

Contents

Introduction

"Dairy free" implies freedom, rather than the loss implied in "dairyless." Although I didn't coin the positive term, I suspect that the person who did knew food and eating should be a good experience. Focusing on the one ingredient missing from a dietary regimen seems depressing, especially when you can enjoy so many other wonderful foods without it. This is my philosophy, and I hope it becomes yours: "dairy free" means the freedom to enjoy other healthier, tasty foods in its place.

Restrictions and obstacles in cooking often make us find other avenues to culinary success. What seems like a dietary limitation at first will set your culinary imagination ablaze. When I was in college, for example, I rolled out dough more than once with a wine bottle because I didn't have a rolling pin, and I somehow felt more satisfied with my pie crust than I ever have with the rolling pin. (Sorry, rolling pin, it's just not the same thrill.) Going dairy free, you'll find foods you now love but might never have tried.

WHY I BECAME DAIRY FREE

I haven't always been dairy free. I was one of those sick kids that seemed to have perpetual digestive distress. "She has a sensitive stomach," my mother used to say. Back in those days, lactose intolerance was just becoming known, and looking for allergies when there was illness wasn't the norm.

In my teenage years, I became vegan and my digestive problems went away. It was a decision I made for the environment more than anything, but I may have also had an inkling that dairy was not good for my body. I started cooking, first as an experimental home cook, then as a prep cook in a restaurant, and then as a line cook and baker. I read anything I could about cooking, trying lots of recipes. I was in love with food, specifically with making vegan food taste delicious. I was dairy free, egg free, and free from animal protein, so I thought that I was on the right track. But my health took a nosedive in my late teens and early twenties from undereating, and I started rethinking my relationship with food and my body. I wanted to reexamine what I so loved about food, and what made me feel so satisfied when I made and shared it with others.

I wanted to turn things around. I was tired of feeling sick. I was inspired by people I knew who lived truly healthy lives. I began a vigorous running routine, and did yoga several times a week. I paid close attention to where my food came from, and I read all I could about health and nutrition. I decided to stop following a strict vegan diet, partially because I loved food and the social aspects of sharing food, and partially because I wanted to eat some animal products. With a history of undereating, I wanted to remove the barriers and restrictions and eat healthy fish and organic eggs.

I, therefore, began eating dairy—what I thought was "healthy" dairy, of course—but soon started having digestive problems all over again. I couldn't figure it out. I had attributed my early digestive problems to processed foods, so I was at a loss as to why I was feeling so sick now. My doctor suggested I may have a food allergy, and a few tests later, he confirmed it: I had been allergic to dairy all along.

Realizing that I had had an allergy all along actually felt like validation. I now knew how to join the healthy club. In my kitchen, taking out the dairy again wasn't a drastic blow. I had been vegan for many years. I knew how to read a label for dairy and cook without it. I soon felt well again, and I began working toward greater personal health, more committed than ever to finding a way to enjoy an alternative diet that was healthy and also didn't make me feel out of place at social gatherings. I cooked and tested and tried, and I adjusted. I shopped and read. I wanted to love my food and for it to treat me well.

Since then, I have written about dairy-free cooking, dairy-free recipes, and the benefits of eating food that promotes good health. I work as a cook-turned–food writer and run a blog called Dairy-Free Cooking on About.com, and I write food articles and reviews for newspapers and magazines. I have created recipes for several restaurants and catered a few weddings, including my own (the recipe for my wedding cake is available online at dairyfreecooking.about.com).

For the most part, I am just like you—looking for ways to cook and bake without an ingredient that has become a staple in today's processed-crazed society, and searching other cuisines for inspiration. I am not a professional chef, doctor, food scientist, or nutritionist. I just like to eat food that makes me feel good, and make food that I feel good about sharing with the people I love.

WHAT YOU'LL FIND IN THIS BOOK

This book offers recipes for not just other cuisines but alternative diets as well. Some are suitable for gluten-free dairy-free diets, and many for dairy-free, soy-free, and vegan diets. I like to make informed decisions about what I put in my body. Sure, I enjoy a slice of Vegan Cheesecake (page 169) now and again, and nothing is as heavenly as a homemade Lemon Meringue Pie (page 162), but I believe that much of the illness that plagues affluent Western cultures can be prevented by better overall eating. Scientific research backs this belief, and I'll share some of the findings with you.

Most of all, however, I want to surprise you. I want to surprise your guests as you tell them that what they ate wasn't actually cheese but something good for them. I want you to see the potential in a handful of almonds and feel victorious over a cracked coconut. I want to share with you what I've learned in my journey—that whole foods are fulfilling nutritionally, so much fun to cook with, delicious, and beautiful from start to finish.

Enjoy your food, and be well!

Chapter 1

MOO'VE OVER, DAIRY: THE DAIRY-FREE LIFESTYLE

I DO NOT LIKE FOCUSING on negatives when it comes to diets—I prefer to focus on the positives of going dairy free. However, there are negatives associated with dairy consumption, and, in particular, the kind of dairy regularly consumed in Western cultures. I intend to review them here and then move on to the positive health effects of substitutes in the chapters to come.

Let's start with the basics of what dairy-free eating means, and why you or someone you love might choose a dairy-free diet.

What Is Dairy Free?

Dairy free means a food or diet does not contain milk from mammals of any kind, including cows, goats, and sheep. (This does not, despite a common misconception, include eggs, which are entirely different proteins.) A study published in the *Journal of Allergy and Clinical Immunology* investigated the cross-sensitization of children with allergies to cow's milk to other mammalian milks and found that these other milks are just as unsafe for people with allergies to cow's milk. Going dairy free is more than just avoiding milks—it's also about avoiding all parts of milk. A dairy-free diet today is more complicated than it would have been centuries ago, but this is because the way we eat in modern societies is complicated.

Because of processed foods, dairy free means more than just avoiding milk and milk-based foods such as butter, cream, and cheese. No milk means avoiding milk proteins such as casein and whey, and lactose, which is the sugar component of dairy. In general, these proteins are the primary allergens for people with allergies to dairy. They and other dairy-derived ingredients are found in countless processed foods, such as store-bought sauces, cereals, breads, snack foods, deli meats, and protein powders, just to name a few. So if you simply avoid whole dairy products but do not read your labels, you are probably inadvertently consuming dairy.

Cooking and eating dairy free doesn't have to be overly complicated, though. Just like any healthy diet regimen or allergy-friendly diet, it comes down to knowing what's in your food and what's not. This begins with reading labels, and relying on fresh vegetables and other whole foods as much as possible.

The dairy-free diet is not a new one, after all; many cultures rarely or never eat dairy in the first place. In the West, however, where we have often prized economy over health and quality when it comes to food, dairy is everywhere. Historians have made the point that in the United States, businesspeople rather than farmers have shaped the dairy industry, much in the same way other conventional agriculture is shaped. The ways that milk and dairy products were enjoyed in the early 1800s, when most families had their own cow, have changed with industrialization and the growth of cities. Now, milk is "manufactured." Cows are injected with antibiotics and hormones and milked by machines, not people. This produces lower-quality milk that is less expensive to mass-produce and sell. Milk is treated like another inexpensive crop that can be used in processed foods. As a result, dairy is everywhere.

Going dairy free in the United States and other Western cultures can seem daunting at first. But take heart. This book and the recipes within will help you realize that going dairy free is easier than you think, especially if you take on a whole-foods approach that embraces countless foods that are naturally dairy free. Going dairy free means many things. It means making a commitment to reading labels, avoiding many processed foods, and asking for alternatives in restaurants, such as requesting that your food be cooked with olive oil instead of butter. It means finding alternative recipes for your favorites, discovering healthier ways to add richness and creamy textures to dishes, and cooking with ingredients that may be new to you. In the end, you'll find yourself enjoying foods and dishes you never would have tried otherwise.

Why Go Dairy Free?

You may be looking for recipes to feed a child or spouse with an allergy, or trying to reduce your dairy intake in the name of overall good health. You may be making an ethical choice to consume fewer animal products or go vegan. So before we delve into the benefits—and there are many—let's look at the reasons to cut the dairy from your diet.

ALLERGIES AND HEALTH CONCERNS

If you, your child, or another family member has a diagnosed allergy to dairy, you're not alone. Dairy is considered a "Top 8" allergen, which means that of all the people with food allergies, a great deal are allergic to dairy. In 2011, a study published in *Pediatrics* indicated that of food-allergic children, dairy is the second most prevalent allergy after peanuts. These allergies and sensitivities are not limited to weaned babies and adults, either. Breast-feeding mothers are finding that if they consume dairy, their babies can be colicky, and some medical experts believe consuming dairy while breast-feeding increases the likelihood of food allergies in children. Author and breast-feeding expert Hilary Jacobsen says in her book, *Mother Food: Foods and Herbs That Promote Milk Production and a Mother's Health,* that exposing an infant to dairy, even through breast milk, increases the infant's sensitivity to dairy and the possibility of developing an allergy. She goes on to say that many infants diagnosed with colic actually improve once the breast-feeding mother removes milk from her diet.

Although lactose intolerance is not the same as a milk allergy, people with lactose intolerance may also look for substitutions to dairy foods and avoid dairy products when possible. A recent study published in the *Journal of the American Dietetic Association* estimates about 25 percent of the U.S. population and 75 percent of the population worldwide have low lactase levels or lactose intolerance, suggesting that, at the very least, dairy products are uncomfortable to consume for many, if not most, people. Though many products on the market make milk more digestible for the lactose intolerant, a growing mountain of evidence suggests that even lactose-free dairy is a contributing factor to debilitating diseases, including autoimmune illnesses, cancer, heart disease, and osteoporosis. Yes, osteoporosis, the one disease that milk is commonly associated with preventing!

Because bone health is directly related to calcium intake, you may assume that consumption of milk—which contains high levels of calcium—would equal better bone health and lower incidences of osteoporosis, right? Not according to several recent studies that indicate that the prevalence of osteoporosis is actually higher in dairy-consuming nations such as the United States, Australia, and New Zealand. In fact, a twelve-year study performed at Harvard on bone density and milk consumption observed 78,000 women and found that those who drank milk three times a day suffered more fractures than those who rarely or never drank milk. Studies like those cited in T. Colin Campbell's *The China Study* indicate that diets that are high in animal protein, including dairy protein, are the cause, not the panacea, for osteoporosis.

The reason seems fairly obvious once parsed: dairy products and other animal proteins increase the metabolic acid load in the body, while calcium acts as a neutralizing agent in the body. So when the body's metabolic acid load climbs, the body uses calcium to neutralize it. What does this mean, exactly? Your body leaches calcium from bones to neutralize acid. Have you ever heard someone tell you that you should drink milk when consuming acidic fruits? This advice isn't all wrong, because the calcium helps neutralize the acid and the vitamin C aids in calcium absorption. But the evidence suggests that for bone health it's better to drink a glass of orange juice that has been fortified with calcium and vitamin D.

Cancer, heart disease, and diabetes, as well as other autoimmune disorders, are now linked to dairy consumption. While the reasons given vary in specifics, the numbers do not. In countries where there is an increase in milk consumption, there is also an increase in cancers, heart disease, type 1 diabetes, and other autoimmune disorders.

Books like Keith Woodford's *Devil in the Milk* contain evidence that the culprit is a dairy protein present in modern milk. Woodford pulls together more than 100 scientific papers that discuss the impacts of a protein fragment found in some dairy cows that is referred to as A1 beta casein. This particular protein has been linked with illnesses such as autism, type 1 diabetes, and heart disease. Not all cows have this protein, but unless dairies screen for it and breed cows that are free from it, any jug of milk you buy at the grocery likely contains this potentially dangerous protein.

Other books and studies claim that consumption of dairy is in part responsible for the onset of these diseases. It is a well-documented fact that the proteins found in cow's milk have the ability to initiate type 1 diabetes, an incurable, lifelong disease that often manifests itself during infancy and childhood. Studies and reviews published in respected health journals such as *The New England Journal of Medicine, Diabetes/ Metabolism Research and Reviews*, and *Current Diabetes Reviews* have pointed to the link between early consumption of cow's milk and the incidence of type 1 diabetes. The rationale behind this linkage has to do with the similarity between cow's-milk proteins and proteins found in the human body. When we ingest a dairy protein, some proteins slip into the bloodstream before breaking down into their amino acid components. Our bodies treat these undigested cow proteins, which are similar to our own, as foreign invaders and create "molds" to destroy them, triggering an autoimmune response that attacks the body's own cells. This is the beginning of diabetes. It is possible that babies with underdeveloped digestive systems who are fed cow's milk-based formula early have a greater risk for these diseases.

The links between various types of cancers and dairy intake have also been well documented. In a 2001 health study review, the researchers stated that one of the "most consistent dietary predictors for prostate cancer" is dairy consumption. One of the mechanisms behind this dietary predictor is the same one that correlates with the incidence of breast cancer: a growth hormone called Insulin-like Growth Factor 1 (IGF-1). According to Campbell, IGF-1 is becoming known as a predictor of cancer the same way cholesterol is a predictor for heart disease. This hormone is responsible for controlling the rate of cell growth in the body. When IGF-1 is present in unhealthy amounts, it speeds the growth of new cells and inhibits the removal of old ones. This leads to cancer. Dairy increases the load of IGF-1 in the blood while simultaneously decreasing our body's stores of vitamin D—a powerful nutrient in preventing cancer—and creates an environment where cancer can thrive.

Last but not least, heart disease is associated with the overconsumption of dairy products. Diets high in cholesterol and saturated fat are proclaimed as recipes for heart disease. Dairy has saturated fats ("bad" saturated fats, as we'll explore later) and cholesterol in spades. So it follows that cultures that consume diets higher in animal and dairy products also have a higher incidence of heart disease than those cultures that subsist more on plant-based foods. A study published in the *European Journal of Clinical Nutrition* found that milk consumption strongly correlated with an increase in blood cholesterol levels and coronary mortality.

Would milk substitutes have the same effect? Coconut milk, for example, has a high saturated-fat content. The difference between the saturated fats found in coconut milk and the fats found in dairy products has to do with the effects on cholesterol. Coconut milk raises the body's HDL, or good cholesterol, not the LDL cholesterol that leads to heart disease. Plant-based proteins such as soy have been shown to lower cholesterol levels, while milk proteins such as casein have been shown to raise them. Another study published in the mid-1990s by Dr. Caldwell B. Esselstyn sought to treat patients with severe heart disease with the introduction of a plant-based dairy-free diet, and the results were astounding. The disease in these patients not only did not accelerate; it was reversed. Those plants are powerful!

That's why, throughout this book, you will find recipes for dishes prepared primarily with plant-based proteins and healthy fats. The evidence that the diseases of affluent societies that consume too much meat and dairy can be prevented and possibly reversed by a nutritionally sound dairy-free regimen is a compelling motivation to try something new.

VEGAN AND ETHICAL REASONS

Although this is not a vegan book, you will find many vegan recipes here. I believe that eating a plant-based diet is a good thing. Purchasing ingredients that are fresh, organic, and local is the healthiest—and most delicious—way to eat. The dairy industry relies heavily on antibiotics, artificial hormones, and factory-farmed cattle, and so by removing the dairy from your diet, you are one step closer to really knowing what's in your food.

No other species than humans relies on dairy as a food source beyond weaning, and no other species relies on another species' milk, ever. Although critics claim that our bodies should be able to naturally digest the milk of other mammals, nothing about the way that large-scale dairy farms operates is natural.

Dr. Robert M. Kradjian has written on this topic, addressing the way that milk is marketed as comforting, the way a mother's milk is to a newborn. The caveat is that the milk people are buying at the supermarket is not mother's milk for a newborn, it is milk intended for newborn calves that adult humans are consuming. "Milk is not just milk," Kradjian says. "The milk of every species of mammal is unique and specifically tailored to the requirements of that animal. For example, cows' milk is much richer in protein than human milk by three to four times as much. It has five to seven times the mineral content. However, it is markedly deficient in essential fatty acids when compared to human mothers' milk. Mothers' milk has six to ten times as much of the essential fatty acids, especially linoleic acid. (Incidentally, skimmed cow's milk has no linoleic acid.) It simply is not designed for humans." In his article, "The Milk Letter: a Message to My Patients," he summarizes more than 500 scientific articles published in a five-year period by stating that none claims milk is an excellent or nutritious food. All the reports discussed milk's correlation to allergies, infections, and disease.

Whatever your reasons for cutting dairy from your diet, know that you're in good company. You're part of the many other countries and cultures that traditionally cook dairy free.

Dairy-Free World

Many cultures in the world rarely—if ever—eat dairy. Instead, these cuisines focus on plant sources like oils, soy, and rich natural milks such as coconut milk, all of which are dairy free, delicious, and easy to cook with. Many Asian and island cuisines—from the Caribbean to the Philippines—rely on coconut milk for sauces, soups, and drinks, as well as coconut oil as a primary fat. In Indian cuisine, some of the richest, creamiest daals are prepared with only lentils, oil, vegetables, and spices. South Africa boasts some of most terrific puddings prepared with only fruit, egg yolks, juice, and flavoring.

Many of my inspirations for the recipes in this book have come from non-Western cuisines, even if the recipes themselves are Western in flavor and presentation. Fermented soy products have inspired many of my cheese substitutes, such as Cashew Blue Cheese (page 62); and agar flakes—derived from seaweed—are my best friend when making hardened vegan cheeses like Homemade Nut Cheeses (pages 58–60). If you are fortunate enough to live near an Asian market, go there and explore. Let your senses guide you, and get excited—there are so many wonderful foods you can eat without dairy.

Chapter 2

HOW TO GO DAIRY FREE (AND STILL GET YOUR CALCIUM!)

DAIRY INGREDIENTS, as we've discussed in the previous chapter, exist in more foods than just dairy products. Butter, cheese, cream, and milk have no part in the dairy-free diet, of course, but neither do other ingredients such as casein, lactose, and whey, all of which are found in processed and prepared foods. In this chapter, we'll examine which ingredients are offenders to the dairy-free diet, and how you can bake and cook delicious foods without them. We'll also discuss one of the biggest nutritional concerns of going dairy free: how to get your calcium.

Common Dairy Ingredients and How to Cook without Them

Butter is a key ingredient in baked goods, breads, desserts, sauces, sautés, and soups. Because it has been used as a food source for thousands of years, it is no wonder that butter is still a foundational ingredient in recipes. On an ingredient label, look out for butter, butter fat, butter oil, butter solids, and ghee, which is another word for clarified butter, and a traditional ingredient in Indian and Middle Eastern cuisines.

Butter adds fat, flavor, and richness to dishes, so to replace it, you need a product that does the same thing. I use soy margarine and other vegetable-based margarines in any recipe that calls for butter. For the healthiest product, look for margarines without hydrogenated fats. In recipes for quick breads, sauces, sautés, and soups, opt for heart-healthy oils like extra-virgin olive oil instead of butter. For baked goods, desserts, sauces, and soups, coconut oil is another healthy option that adds a delicious flavor and body to any dish. Its only caveat is that it is expensive, so if you are able to buy it in bulk or at wholesale, it is worthwhile to do so.

Avoiding unhealthy fats such as butter gives you the opportunity to add healthy fats in its stead, like extra-virgin olive oil. It is high in phenols, which are powerful antioxidants, and also high in monounsaturated fats that lower LDL ("bad" cholesterol) and raise HDL ("good" cholesterol). Coconut oil, as I'll discuss in chapter 5 (page 37), is loaded with benefits, including antimicrobial, antiviral, heart-helping ones.

Cheese, whether melted, shredded, powdered, or served by itself, is used in countless dishes in Western cuisines. Solid at room temperature, but able to stretch and melt when heated without turning into liquid, cheese is in a class of its own. Without a doubt, it is the dairy product most difficult to imitate.

Buying store-bought dairy-free cheeses can be challenging. Many so-called "nondairy" cheeses are not dairy free but contain casein, whey, or both. Many are also loaded with the processed ingredients you're trying to avoid on a whole-foods diet, so be selective in what you buy. Or to avoid the long list of processed ingredients altogether, make your own. Read the ingredients labels carefully and, as always, opt for products prepared without hydrogenated fats.

Ingredients crucial in making your own dairy-free cheese at home may seem unusual, but are easy to use. Nutritional yeast has been a key ingredient in vegan cuisine for decades because of its naturally cheesy, yeasty flavor. It is easy to find even in mainstream groceries across the United States, and it is a nutritional powerhouse, containing one day's worth of vitamins B_6 and B_{12} in just 2 tablespoons (16 g). Sprinkle it on salads and pasta in place of Parmesan, or use it in your own homemade cheese such as Cashew Cheese (page 58) or Brazil Nut Cheese (page 59).

Agar, seaweed that acts as a vegetarian gelatin substitute, is a wonder in dairy-free cheese making. By adding agar to liquid and simmering before adding to the remaining ingredients, it creates a pliable texture similar to that found in cheese products. Agar flakes are sold at health food stores, Asian markets, and specialty groceries. It is expensive, but a little goes a long way, and it's good for you—agar is a good natural source of calcium, iron, and fiber.

Nuts—especially cashews—are the main ingredients in my favorite dairy-free cheeses. Once blended, they create a creamy base for any kind of cheese. Seasonings, nutritional yeast, dairy-free milk like coconut milk, and agar flakes complete the creation. Using these ingredients means that, unlike traditional cheese, homemade dairy-free cheeses contain healthy fats, vital nutrients, protein, and flavor.

Soft cheeses, such as cottage cheese, ricotta, and yogurt cheese, are easy to make dairy free. Using tofu in place of cottage cheese and ricotta is a healthy, inexpensive, and tasty substitution. Use dairy-free soft cheeses in place of ricotta in pasta dishes, or serve with fruit. Make dairy-free yogurt cheese with any unsweetened, plain dairy-free yogurt, a bowl, a cooling rack, and cheesecloth. Stir a pinch or two of salt into the tub of dairy-free yogurt. Place cheesecloth over the top and pull it taut, then secure the cheesecloth with a rubber band. Turn the tub upside down on top of a cooling rack set over a bowl. The liquid from the yogurt drains into the bowl for several days until what remains is the firm part of the yogurt, or the cheese. Enjoy it with crackers or veggies as a healthy snack.

Cream, a common ingredient in sauces, soups, desserts, and morning coffee, goes by many names, including clotted cream, crème fraîche, half-and-half, heavy whipping cream, and sour cream. All cream originates from butterfat skimmed from the surface of milk. In other words: creams of any kind are fatty. What they add to each dish varies a great deal, so what you choose to replace these with will vary as well. Half-and-half can be replaced with soy-based half-and-half or any milk alternative in your morning coffee. Sour cream replacement is easy with soy-based sour cream or homemade dairy-free sour cream such as Coconut Sour Cream (page 57). If you need a sour cream substitute for baking, mix $2/3$ cup (160 mL) of any dairy-free milk substitute with 1 tablespoon (15 mL) fresh lemon juice to add that sour flavor and aid the baking agents in rising. Make whipped cream with coconut cream and a pinch of powdered sugar, such as the Coconut Whipped Cream I dollop on my Super-Thick Milkshakes (page 168).

Milk is the first product we usually think of when we think of dairy, because it is the main product from which everything else derives. Milk from any mammal—cows, goats, sheep, etc.—is off-limits to the dairy-free diner, as are buttermilk, buttermilk solids, dry milk powder, dry milk solids, evaporated milk, hydrolyzed milk protein, milk fat, milk powder, milk protein, milk solids, and sweetened condensed milk.

Replacing milk in cereal or puddings is easy because of the dairy-free milks available today. Substitute almond milk, coconut milk, hemp milk, rice milk, and soymilk in any recipe that calls for milk. Experiment with different varieties and find the one that suits you the best. You can also make all of these kinds of milk at home (page 49– 56). Some milk substitutes work better for particular uses. Almond milk is great in morning cereal, while coconut milk makes luscious soups, puddings, and dairy-free cheeses. Soymilk and hemp milk are both lovely in a latte, and rice milk is terrific for children with multiple allergies.

To replace buttermilk in any recipe, use any dairy-free milk and add 1 tablespoon (15 mL) of lemon juice or apple cider vinegar per 1 cup (235 mL) of milk. Stir to combine and let sit for a minute or so to thicken.

There are two ways to replace evaporated milk for any recipe. One is to pour three times as much dairy-free milk as you need for the recipe into a saucepan (e.g., 3 cups [705 mL] of soymilk for 1 cup [235 mL] of evaporated milk) and simmer on the stove until the milk is reduced to the desired amount. The other method is to combine soymilk powder or rice milk powder with the same amount of water and combine in a blender until smooth.

Powdered milk is simple to replace by using the same amount of soymilk powder, rice milk powder, or potato milk powder. These are sold in health food stores, specialty stores, and online. Coconut milk powder almost always contains casein or a casein derivative, but there are rumors of a vegan coconut milk powder under development, so this may be a possible substitute in coming years.

To replace sweetened condensed milk in a recipe, use the same amount of canned cream of coconut (widely available), which is essentially stabilized sweetened coconut milk. I make my own cream of coconut by refrigerating several unopened cans of coconut milk overnight, draining the liquid from the cans, and scooping out the cream into a small saucepan. I add $1/4$ cup (50 g) unrefined cane sugar per cup of coconut cream, bring the cream to a simmer, and cook over medium heat until the milk is reduced by half. While this second method also works with soymilk or rice milk, the creaminess of the coconut cream makes it the best substitute.

Yogurt is another dairy product that has been eaten for thousands of years. Today it is served on its own, whipped into sauces and dips, frozen into ice cream, or used to coat dried fruit and other snacks. Other words for yogurt that you'll see in the store and on the label are kefir, yogurt cultures, and yogurt powder. In restaurants, raita and tzatziki are common yogurt-based sauces.

Of all dairy products, yogurt probably has the most health benefits because of its probiotic content, but substituting yogurt is easy. The first soymilk yogurt was made over a hundred years ago and sold commercially in Paris in 1911. Large grocery chains now sell almond yogurt, coconut milk yogurt, and soymilk yogurt. Making your own yogurt, such as Almond Yogurt (page 64), at home is simple with dairy-free milk, live cultures, and an inexpensive yogurt maker. You can purchase live, vegan cultures in specialty health food stores and online to use as a starter. To make your dairy-free yogurt without a yogurt maker, as I like to do with my Coconut Yogurt (page 66), all you'll need is dairy-free milk, some dairy-free yogurt to start, a slow cooker, and a cooking thermometer.

Hidden Dairy, from Casein to Whey

Because of the way manufacturers process food today, they are able to isolate parts of milk instead of using the whole product. As a result, several components of milk are present in processed foods, from cereals and snack foods to deli meats and sauces. Some are used to enhance flavor, others act as emulsifying or stabilizing agents, or are used to create that "stretchy" cheese texture in "nondairy" (but not dairy-free) cheeses. Here are the ingredients to look out for while label reading:

Casein is a milk phosphoprotein that is found in the curd, or the part of milk that forms chunks in dairy products such as cottage cheese. Many processed foods use it as a binding or emulsifying agent. It is also the protein to which most milk-allergic persons are allergic. You'll find casein in boxed dinners, frozen meals, soups, energy bars, snack foods, nondairy cheeses, nondairy creamers, and supplements. Look for casein while reading labels, as well as words that contain the word *casein* within them, such as ammonium caseinate, calcium caseinate, casein hydrolysate, iron caseinate, magnesium caseinate, paracasein, potassium caseinate, rennet casein, sodium caseinate, and zinc caseinate. Recaldent, a casein derivative, is sometimes used in chewing gum.

Lactose, the sugar component of milk, is a disaccharide that many adults and children cannot digest due to an insufficient amount of lactase, the enzyme responsible for digesting lactose, in the body. Although people with a dairy allergy are not commonly allergic to lactose, the presence of lactose in a food means it is not suitable for the lactose intolerant or milk allergic. Usually, if lactose is present, another dairy ingredient is also involved, but not always. Lactose improves the water-holding capacity of deli meats, and enhances browning in baked goods.

Whey, the other main protein in milk, is the watery or liquid part of dairy products (like in the Little Bo Peep nursery rhyme—"curds and whey"). Whey is another ingredient that can trigger an allergic reaction in those allergic to dairy. Many processed food products contain whey, including sport protein drinks and whey protein powders. Two of whey's derivatives, lactalbumin and lactoglobulin, are stabilizing agents in food products and health supplements. When whey is crystallized, it creates a high-lactose powder that manufacturers add to baked goods, confections, and infant formulas. Any of the following, when listed on a food label, indicates the presence of dairy: sweet whey, whey powder, whey protein concentrate, and whey protein hydrolysate.

The easiest way to avoid consuming hidden dairy is to read labels. The easiest way to know what's in your food—and know that it's healthy—is to pass on the processed stuff and rely on whole foods.

Nondairy Calcium Sources

The milk industry has done a great job of linking milk consumption with calcium consumption and bone health, and as a result, people often assume that if you are not drinking milk, you will not consume enough calcium. But let's think for a moment: where do cows get their calcium? Grass. That's right—from a plant. What's more, as we discussed in the first chapter, milk-consuming countries actually have higher incidences of osteoporosis. Several recent studies, such as the twelve-year study at Harvard that observed that women who drank the most milk suffered the most bone fractures, have discovered that milk is not the bone-health wonder food that we have been led to believe. As the advertisements ask, even if you've "Got milk?" (and possibly because you've "Got milk"), you may still get osteoporosis.

It's true that calcium is important for overall good health as well as bone health. Calcium is essential in the formation of strong bones and teeth, and it also lowers cholesterol levels and participates in other bodily functions directly related to heart and brain health.

So how can you get your calcium without dairy?

Tofu is one of the best dairy-free sources of calcium, packing in almost 400 milligrams of calcium—about 40 percent of the daily value recommendation—per 4-ounce (112 g) serving. Crumble your tofu over a salad, whip up a batch of Tofu Ricotta (page 63) for a pasta dish, or bake, fry, or scramble your tofu into something delicious, inexpensive, and healthy.

Leafy greens are up there, too. One cup (30 g) of cooked spinach or collard greens will give you about 25 percent of your daily value of calcium. One cup of cooked kale, mustard greens, or Swiss chard (30 g) will yield almost 10 percent. Instead of preparing a salad with romaine lettuce, which will give you only about 3 percent of your daily calcium needs, steam some calcium-rich greens instead, and then drizzle them with a little bit of heart-healthy olive oil and fresh lemon juice.

Blackstrap molasses, another nutrient-dense, calcium-rich food, is one of the easiest to add to your daily dietary routine. Just 2 teaspoons (14 g) of blackstrap molasses contains about 11 percent of your daily calcium needs as well as other vital nutrients such as iron, potassium, and magnesium. Best of all, it tastes great. Add a teaspoon to a morning smoothie or cup of tea, or just take a teaspoon here and there throughout the day. For a special seasonal treat, make the molasses-rich Gingerbread with Vanilla Glaze (page 156), and boast that it's good for you.

Just ¼ cup (36 g) of **almonds** will give you about 90 mg of calcium, in addition to about 6 g of protein and 3 g of fiber. Almonds, as you'll see on page 26, are dairy-free wunderkinds. Use almonds to make dairy-free cheese, dairy-free milk, or your own dairy-free yogurt. They also make one of the healthiest on-the-go snacks; just grab a handful and hit the road.

A quarter cup (36 g) of **sesame seeds** provides nearly 35 percent of the daily recommended value of calcium, so don't overlook these little seeds. Sprinkle them on salads, or purchase tahini made from whole seeds (not hulled seeds or kernels)

SUBSTITUTING DAIRY-FREE MILKS IN RECIPES

Some milk substitutes work better in certain recipes than others. Coconut milk makes soups, puddings, and sauces creamy, and it's the best milk to use to make dairy-free whipped cream and sour cream. Almond milk, brown rice milk, cashew milk, and soymilk are terrific milks for everyday uses, such as adding to a batter, pouring over cereal, or drinking straight from the glass. Because soymilk is similar to milk in protein and calorie content, it is a safe replacement choice for almost any recipe.

When selecting dairy-free milk for a given recipe, consider what you're looking to replace. Coconut milk and coconut cream replace whole-fat dairy beautifully in milk, whipped cream, crème fraîche, and sour cream. Almond milk and cashew milk are both mellow in flavor but add a hint of richness and body to soups and sauces. Use them to replace 1% or 2% milk. Brown rice milk is thin and sweet, so it replaces skim milk well.

Keep the people you're serving in mind, too. Brown rice milk is hypoallergenic, so for large groups with varied diets, it's often the safest choice. Coconut milk is next, as it's probably the milk that goes over best with people who are used to consuming rich foods.

The more you experiment, the more you'll come to know which milk will work best for a given recipe. To start, try some of the recipes in this book.

and use in homemade hummus, salad dressings, or as a sandwich spread. Tahini is an ingredient in some of my dairy-free cheese sauces and dips (Cashew Cheese Dip, page 94, for example), and you can even substitute tahini for peanut butter in peanut butter cookies to add an extra dose of calcium and a special flavor to your sweets.

Basil, thyme, and **oregano** are all excellent sources of calcium and easy to add to any savory dish. Just 2 teaspoons (3 g) of these herbs dried provide about 5 percent of your daily value of calcium. Create a fresh tomato–herb sauce for a pasta dish, add herbs to your homemade dairy-free cheeses, or prepare the Vegan Basil Pesto (page 136) and use with pasta, on pizza, or on sandwiches. No need to eat dried or fresh herbs by the handful; sprinkling a little here and there can contribute to your daily calcium intake.

If you are looking for a calcium-rich sweet treat, you need look no further than a few dried **figs.** One cup (150 g) of dried figs provides as much calcium as 1 cup (235 mL) of skim milk, as well as fiber, magnesium, and potassium. Chop up dried figs to add to your morning oatmeal, sprinkle on a salad or rice dish, or make a special appetizer like figs stuffed with Cashew Blue Cheese (page 62). Figs are nutritionally dense and caloric, but added sparingly to your diet can contribute to your daily nutrition and calcium intake.

Scallops are rich in calcium, with about 130 mg per 4-ounce (112 g) serving. In addition to calcium, scallops are a good source of protein, B vitamins, iron, and magnesium. Scallops cook very quickly, so searing, sautéing, or broiling are the best ways to prepare these little mollusks. Use a bit of heart-healthy olive oil to keep your scallops from sticking to your pan or dish while cooking, and serve with vegetables, brown rice, or pasta. Scallops are high in cholesterol, and shellfish is a "Top 8" allergen, so if you are eating a low-cholesterol diet or avoiding all primary allergens, scallops may not be for you.

Broccoli provides about 42 mg of calcium (4 percent daily value) per cup (71 g) and can be a simple, nutritious side dish or salad. Blanch broccoli in hot water or steam for just a minute or two until it is bright green and tender-crisp. Serve as is or with a pinch of salt and pepper, or add broccoli to rice dishes, pasta dishes, and casseroles.

When creating a healthy diet plan, moderation and variety are key. Nutrients react with one another, so a healthy diet regimen will not lean too heavily on any one food or nutrient but will include foods from multiple sources on a daily basis. Vitamin C, vitamin D, and magnesium all contribute to proper absorption of calcium, and excessive amounts of caffeine, oxalic acid, protein, sodium, and sugar interferes with absorption. Taking calcium with iron lessens the positive effects of both nutrients, and taking too much zinc will interfere with calcium absorption and vice versa. To make sure that you are getting adequate amounts of calcium and other nutrients, think variety.

Calcium is in a lot of foods besides dairy. That bunch of spinach, handful of almonds, and the block of tofu you've wanted to cook with but maybe haven't known how to all contain simple, healthy solutions to the dairy free conundrum. Ignore the hype, and try to retrain your brain against feeling like your missing out on something—nutritionally or otherwise—when it comes to eating dairy free.

Calcium Facts at a Glance

The National Institutes of Health recommends that adults ages 19 to 50 consume 1,000 mg of calcium per day. Children ages 9 to 18 are advised to consume 1,300 mg per day. Adult women ages 51 to 70 and all adults over 71 are advised to consume 1,200 mg per day.

Vitamin D is essential in the absorption and utilization of calcium, but the form of vitamin D that we take in from food and supplements must first be converted by the liver and the kidneys before it is fully active. Getting some sun—between 5 and 30 minutes of sun exposure at least twice a week between prime sunlight hours of 10 a.m. and 3 p.m., according to the National Institutes of Health— is a healthy way to get sufficient vitamin D. When the skin is exposed to sunlight, a compound in the skin triggers vitamin D synthesis in the body. Fish liver oils, salmon, egg yolks, and fortified orange juice are all good sources as well.

High intakes of **alcohol, caffeine, protein, sodium,** and **sugar** contribute to the urinary loss of calcium, so eating a diet that only includes these in moderation is the best way to ensure you're getting the most nutrients from your food.

Oxalic acid—an organic compound found in some plant-based foods such as almonds, beet greens, kale, rhubarb, soybeans, and spinach—can interfere with calcium absorption. According to Dr. Balch, author of *Prescription for Nutritional Healing,* "casual consumption" of foods containing oxalic acid is not problematic, but overindulgence of foods containing oxalic acid can inhibit proper absorption.

Magnesium is important in maintaining the right balance of calcium in the body, which is why these supplements are often taken together. However, if you take too much, it can compete with calcium.

Moderate exercise promotes calcium absorption, but excessive exercise inhibits it. Weight-bearing exercise has been shown to increase bone density in several studies such as one published in the *Journal of the American Medical Association,* but excessive exercise is shown to decrease it. In all things, moderation!

DAIRY-FREE COOKING EQUIPMENT

Cooking dairy-free foods is easiest if you invest in the proper tools. Although you can make most of the recipes in this book with just a $30 blender, cheesecloth, wooden spoons, and some pans, a few additional pieces of equipment are worth looking into.

A high-powdered professional blender makes grinding nuts for homemade dairy-free cheeses, pureeing soups, and whipping up smoothies a breeze. A good blender will cost you upwards of $300, but if you are grinding nuts on a daily basis, it can be worth it. (If you opt for a cheaper blender, just keep the warranty—you will use it.) Using an everyday blender means a bit more work on your part, too. When grinding nuts, making homemade cheeses, or pureeing vegetables for soup, take care to stop the blender and scrape down the sides periodically to ensure even blending.

An ice cream maker seems like a luxury item, but it's something you'll use regularly if you have one in your kitchen. An inexpensive $50 to $75 ice cream maker will yield a professional-level product, and it's much easier than blending your ice cream, placing it in the freezer, blending again, placing it in the freezer, and so on.

Immersion blenders are useful for pureed soups and sauces, minimizing mess and preparation time, and they are very affordable. They are not a necessity, but if you prepare pureed soups on a regular basis and don't look forward to cleaning the blender and an extra pot, you'll be happy you have one.

Nut-milk bags are sold at specialty and health food stores and will save you money on cheesecloth. They're reusable, which reduces on waste, and they last for many uses. Use them to make any of the homemade milks in this book in place of cheesecloth.

A yogurt maker, like an ice cream maker, makes life easier when it comes to making homemade yogurt. Good-quality yogurt makers cost $40 to $80. You can make your own homemade yogurt, such as Coconut Yogurt (page 66), in a slow cooker, but a yogurt maker provides the ideal conditions in which to ferment your yogurt and results in a product most similar to the original, especially for thinner alternative milks such as almond and soy.

Foods to Keep in the Dairy-Free Kitchen

Agar flakes and **agar powder** are useful ingredients for making dairy-free cheese. Agar, a gelatin substitute, helps solidify your homemade dairy-free cheeses. It's also a good source of calcium, iron, and fiber (agar is actually 80 percent fiber). To see how it's used in your own kitchen, try making any of the dairy-free nut cheeses in this book (pages 58–62).

Almonds make one of my favorite milk substitutes, and they're a great source of calcium, so keep some around for homemade Almond Milk (page 49) and just for snacking.

Avocados are great sources of healthy fats. They add a creamy texture to savory dairy-free dishes and desserts, such as Cashew Cheese–Stuffed Jalapeño Poppers (page 96), Avocado Mac n' Cheese (page 171), and Raw Avocado Cheesecake (page 163). Avocados are the main ingredient in guacamole, a simple—and immensely popular—dairy-free, gluten-free, soy-free vegan snack, served with veggies like cucumber slices and carrots or organic corn chips.

Block-style tofu makes a lovely substitute for soft cheeses such as ricotta (page 63), and **silken tofu** is easily whipped up into tofu mayo (page 138), a cheese sauce for Better Eggplant Parmesan (page 118), and custardlike desserts such as Chocolate Peanut Butter Pie (page 151).

Canned coconut milk is useful for many dairy-free recipes. Keep several cans in the refrigerator for Coconut Sour Cream (page 57), Coconut Milk Whipped Cream (page 168), pureed soups such as Cream of Mushroom Soup (page 109), and extra-special desserts like Coconut Crème Brûlée (page 152). Refrigerating the coconut milk allows the milk to separate so that the cream can be easily used in recipes.

Cashews are my favorite nuts for homemade cheeses such as Cashew Cheese (page 58), nut-based sauces, and nut-based creams. They blend easily without soaking, and when soaked, they make the most creamy, delightful treat.

Coconut oil is expensive, but once you've started using it, you'll never stop. Spread it on toast for a healthy substitute for butter or margarine, use it in the recipes calling for coconut oil in this book, or make your own margarine (page 68). Coconut oil can be used exactly like butter, although coconut oil becomes very hard when cold—much harder than butter or margarine. So if using it in place of butter in a pie crust (such as in the Savory Spinach–Broccoli Pie, page 130), don't refrigerate your dough for more than the recommended amount of time or it will need to rest for a long time before you're able to roll it out. Likewise, if a recipe calls for room temperature, warm, or melted coconut oil, or for other ingredients to be warm or melted, don't ignore this recommendation.

Extra-virgin olive oil is a super-healthy fat for baked goods and sautés. Like coconut oil, good-quality extra-virgin olive oil isn't cheap, but you get what you pay for. Never skimp when it comes to buying oils. Cheap, refined oils aren't good for you, compared to the healthy unrefined oils loaded with vitamins, antioxidants, and essential fatty acids, such as olive oil.

Nonhydrogenated soy margarine is a quick and easy store-bought substitute for butter that works especially well in baking recipes. Read the label to make sure that your selection is organic non-GMO, and contains no hydrogenated or trans fats.

Nutritional yeast has been the answer to that "missing something" in vegan cheeses for decades. With a naturally cheesy flavor, B vitamins, protein, and virtually no fat, it's a win–win ingredient, and a little bit goes a long way when it comes to taste. Nutritional yeast, not to be confused with brewers' yeast, can be found in the bulk sections of regular groceries and health food stores alike.

Whole coconuts may seem intimidating at first, but after you've cracked a few, you'll be hooked. While canned coconut milk is useful for many things, especially as substitutes for sour cream and whipped cream, there is nothing like making your own. Try Raw Coconut Milk (page 50) for a refreshing treat and Better-Than-Canned Coconut Milk (page 52) for a creamy, flavorful milk that tastes great.

What's the Difference Between "Nondairy" and "Dairy Free"?

Reading labels is important for keeping a dairy-free diet, especially because terms such as "dairy free" and "nondairy" can be misleading. There is no actual Food and Drug Administration (FDA) regulatory term for "dairy-free" products, so although products are usually dairy free, read labels anyway to make sure.

The FDA has, however, established regulations for the term "non-dairy," but they were established more to protect the dairy industry than dairy-free diets. According to the Food Allergy Research and Resource Program at the University of Nebraska, the term "non-dairy" is a "long-standing byproduct of the strong dairy lobby that wanted to assure that substitute milk and cream products could not bear the dairy name." (This is also the same lobbying group that claims that using the word "milk" on soymilk and other alternative milk products is misbranding.) Legally, goods bearing the term "nondairy" cannot be whole dairy products or contain whole dairy products such as milk, but they can contain dairy derivatives, such as caseinates. Because milk is an allergen, the product will still indicate that it contains milk derivatives on the ingredients label, which is why reading the label—and not just grabbing a product that claims to be "nondairy"—is imperative.

Chapter 3

ALMONDS: THE DAIRY-FREE WUNDERKIND

FIRST, IT WAS SOY: soymilk, soy yogurt, and soy ice cream. Then, as we'll discuss in the following chapter, soy became a controversial topic and consumers became more cautious about consuming it. Rice milk, although offering plenty of health benefits, wasn't thick enough. Coconut milk was too thick or too nutty for some recipes. Almond milk, with its mellow flavor, milk-white color, and milk-like consistency, was just right.

As a result, almond-based products boomed in the past decade. Almond milks, almond yogurts, almond ice cream, almond puddings, you name it—almond products have taken over the shelves. As you'll see, almonds are bases for some of

the most fantastic homemade dairy-free recipes, including Almond Cheese (page 60), Vanilla Almond Ice Cream (page 172), Almond Yogurt (page 64), and Almond Milk (page 49). What's more, almonds are possibly one of the healthiest foods on earth.

Replacing dairy with almonds is a step toward good health. While many properties of dairy are linked to illness and poor health, almonds have been shown to prevent, and in some cases improve, these same illnesses. Comprised of fiber, healthy fats, protein, and various health-promoting phytochemicals and nutrients, almonds are tiny nutritional powerhouses with tons of flavorful potential.

Benefits of Almonds—The Skinny on Fats, Fiber, and Health

A common—but not factual—objection to nuts is their fat content. It's true that almonds are high in fat, but it's the good kind: monounsaturated fats. Although unhealthy fats like those found in dairy have been shown to increase the incidence of heart problems and weight gain, the opposite is true with almond fats. Studies across the board show that the monounsaturated fat content in almonds lowers LDL (bad) cholesterol levels and reduces risk of coronary heart disease. Dairy fats, on the other hand, raise LDL cholesterol, as evidenced by a 2010 article that reviewed more than seventy studies on dairy products and plasma cholesterol levels.

An article published in 2006 in the *Journal of Nutrition* cites several large epidemiological studies that conclude that nuts, including almonds, have a protective effect on coronary heart disease. Another study published in the *International Journal of Obesity* evaluated the role almonds may play in weight loss. It concluded that an almond-enriched low-calorie diet "has a potential role in reducing the public health implications of obesity." Participants in the study who ate an almond-enriched low-calorie diet experienced more weight loss and more sustained weight loss than the control group, which ate a low-calorie diet enriched with complex carbohydrates.

Almonds may be fatty, but in an otherwise healthy diet they protect our hearts and may also prevent weight gain, not cause it. By contrast, studies have linked obesity with milk consumption. A recent Harvard Medical School study examined more than 12,000 children and found that children who consume more than three servings of milk each day are 35 percent more likely to become obese.

Almonds may also be helpful for people at risk for developing diabetes, due in part to their good fats. A study published in the *Journal of the American College of Nutrition* concluded that a diet consisting of 20 percent almonds over a period of sixteen weeks improved insulin sensitivity in subjects. The study included two groups of prediabetic adults. One group received a low-carbohydrate diet that excluded all nuts, while the other consumed a diet of 20 percent almonds (approximately 2 ounces [57 g] per day). The authors concluded that the combination of healthy fats and high fiber content made almonds effective in lowering insulin resistance. Another study published in *Metabolism* went further to demonstrate that when almonds are consumed with simple-carbohydrate foods (white bread in the case of the study), a dose-dependent reduction of the glycemic impact of the carbohydrates occurs when eaten with the almonds. So, the more almonds people ate with simple carbohydrates, the less their blood sugar spiked.

Several studies also suggest that almonds may reduce cancer risk because of one or all of their nutritional properties. A study published in *Cancer Letters* in 2001 found that almonds reduced the risk of colon cancer in rats because of one of the lipid (fat) components in almonds. Almonds also contain about 3 g of fiber per ounce (23 g), which makes them friendly to the digestive process and links almonds with even more risk reductions for a number of conditions, including cancer. An article published in the *Journal of the American Dietetic Association* reviewed forty epidemiological studies that clearly demonstrate a link between more dietary fiber and less cancer. So grab a hand of almonds and get some fiber.

Almonds are high in vitamin E, which is associated with preventing cancer and cardiovascular disease, and promoting healthy skin and hair and preventing cell damage. Almonds and almond oil relieve skin conditions like acne, and studies show that consumption of dairy products, which contain almost no vitamin E, can cause them. Although you can take a vitamin or health supplement such as vitamin E for most properties found in almonds, studies show that relying on a varied whole-foods diet composed of balanced nutrients may be a better option, and that taking supplements of these nutrients creates an imbalance that can do more harm than good. A study published in 2011 in the *Journal of the National Cancer Institute* investigated the role that vitamin E, the kind found in both foods and supplements, may play in preventing cancer, and found that the vitamin in both forms played a role in preventing liver cancer. However, another study (called the SELECT study), published the same year, found that when taken in high doses such as those found in supplements, vitamin E increased the risk of prostate cancer. According to dietician Joseph Gonzales with the Physicians Committee for Responsible Medicine, this is not necessarily because of the vitamin E but because of how people took it. "Vitamin E works in concert with vitamin C in natural whole-food sources to quench free radicals and protect DNA. When you take one nutrient out and synthesize it chemically, it just doesn't seem to work the same as the natural food." Although vitamin E is an essential nutrient found in a bottle, it may be more beneficial to obtain it through a whole-food source such as almonds.

As discussed in the previous chapter, almonds are loaded with other health-boosting nutrients such as calcium, magnesium, and phosphorous, all essential to a healthy diet and important to a dairy-free one. Magnesium assists in the body's uptake of calcium, which is essential to many functions in the body. Almonds contain almost 100 mg of magnesium per ¼ cup (36 g), while whole milk contains only 24 mg per cup (235 mL). A study published in *Osteoporosis International* links magnesium depletion with osteoporosis, and another published in *American Heart Journal* links magnesium deficiency with coronary heart disease risk.

Phosphorous is another key player in bone health, as well as in the use of vitamins and energy conversion. Dr. Balch, author of the best-selling book *Prescription for Nutritional Healing*, advises that "a proper balance of magnesium, calcium, and phosphorous should be maintained at all times. If one of these minerals is present either in excessive or insufficient amounts, this will have adverse effects on the body." Having a balanced diet of whole foods is the best way to ensure that you consume the proper balance of nutrients.

Nut Allergies

Like dairy, tree nuts are also a "Top 8" allergen. According to the Food Allergy and Anaphylaxis Network, an estimated 1.8 million people in the United States are allergic to tree nuts such as almonds. These allergies, like peanut allergies, tend to be lifelong conditions that can have severe reactions, including anaphylaxis. Because of the risk of cross-contamination between tree nut varieties, many people who are allergic to one variety avoid the others as well. For those who are allergic to dairy and almonds or other tree nuts, coconut (which is not a tree nut but a palm fruit), rice, and soy are good alternatives.

If the research in this chapter and those before it have demonstrated anything, it's that Hippocrates was right when he said, "Let food be thy medicine, and medicine be thy food." By eating whole, unprocessed foods that are good for us, we can prevent illness and disease and promote overall good health. Isolating certain foods and minerals and consuming these to excess doesn't work. So as we continue to learn about healthier substitutes, we should keep in mind that even these foods should be a part of a moderate diet.

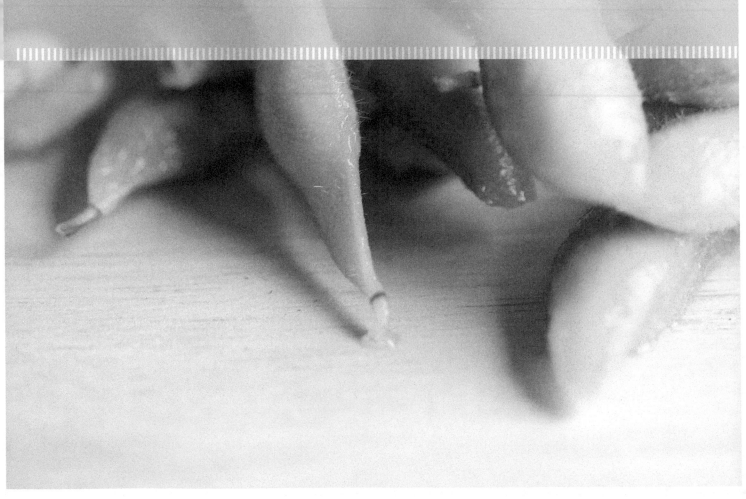

Chapter 4

TO SOY OR NOT TO SOY

IF YOU ARE CONFUSED by the myriad articles and studies published on soy, it's probably because scientists and nutritionists do not have a clear consensus. One week, an article goes viral claiming that soy is the healthiest food on earth, and then the next week, another article says that soy and the soy industry are evil. One article claims that soy prevents cancer, while another claims that soy is carcinogenic. With these kinds of conflicting information, it's difficult for consumers to know what to buy. This chapter explores both sides of the controversy, looking specifically at the research and the opinions of experts, many of whom seem to have reached the same conclusion—that moderation is key.

What the Research Says

The evidence on both sides of the soy debate is compelling but highly contradictory. Research that advocates soy as a health food makes claims that soy lowers cholesterol, prevents cancer, boosts survival in breast cancer patients, is heart healthy, protects against postmenopausal osteoporosis, improves vaginal health in postmenopausal women, and is an easily digested protein source packed with nutrients. Anti-soy advocates claim that soy promotes breast cancer growth, causes hypothyroidism and cancer, may cause pancreatic disorders, inhibits iron absorption, disturbs menstrual cycles in premenopausal women, and may reduce hair growth.

Because of these wildly differing claims, many nutritionists, doctors, and authors have come to a place of cautious indifference on soy. While there may be positive and negative side effects to the food, they are unwilling to claim that soy is either panacea or poison. The point, according to some, is that it is most likely neither.

Kathleen DesMaisons, Ph.D., has conducted extensive research on the subject, including filtering through nearly 500 abstracts and articles on the soy controversy. She still concludes in her writing that there are good sides and bad sides to soy consumption. The same is true of Jonny Bowden, Ph.D., author of *The 150 Healthiest Foods on Earth*, who says he is not a "big fan of soy," largely because of the junk-food soy that we regularly consume in the United States. It's the overprocessed soy cheeses, the soy additives in processed foods, the hydrogenated soy margarines, not necessarily soy itself, that bother him. Marion Nestle, author of the award-winning book *What to Eat*, writes that "the degree of benefit or harm from soy must be too small to make much difference in health. At the moment, it is not possible to prove that soy has any special health benefits beyond minor effects on cholesterol lowering. It is also not possible to prove that soy is perfectly safe." So what do the studies say?

SOY, BREAST CANCER, AND REPRODUCTIVE EFFECTS

The biggest controversy about soy has to do with cancer, and specifically breast cancer. The claims on both sides are based on the presence of organic compounds called isoflavones found in soy products. Soy isoflavones, called phytoestrogens, are estrogenic compounds that mimic behavior of the hormone estrogen in the body. Women with heightened levels of estrogen or longer reproductive cycles (earlier menarche and later menopause) have been associated with a higher risk for developing breast cancer. Some believe these phytoestrogens behaving like estrogens in the body could be carcinogenic, especially for women with other risk factors.

However, the abundance of research does not support this hypothesis. An article published in 2012 in *The New York Times* cites a study that showed that phytoestrogens like those in soy stimulate the growth of breast cancer cells in the lab, but in human studies, such as the one published in *Journal of the American Medical Association* in 2009, the opposite was true. According to this study, "among women with breast cancer, soy food consumption was significantly associated with decreased risk of death and recurrence." In other words, women with breast cancer who consumed soy had *less* risk of dying from breast cancer or from developing cancer again. Another study published in the *British Journal of Cancer* (2008) reviews the results of eight studies that demonstrate that soy food intake might have protective effects against breast cancer. The article concludes that the data from these studies "show a dose-dependent, statistically significant association between soy food intake and breast cancer reduction." According to the data, there was a 16 percent risk reduction per intake of 10 mg soy isoflavones per day.

So according to the studies, not only does soy have the ability to potentially help women with breast cancer survive cancer, but it has a preventative effect as well. Despite the hypothesis that soy's phytoestrogen content may promote breast cancer, studies have not shown that this is the case.

In *The China Study*, performed by Dr. Campbell, rats given high doses of carcinogens and fed a diet of 20 percent protein derived from casein developed early cancer cells. But those fed a diet of 20 percent protein derived from soy did not, even though they were given the same high level of carcinogen. In other words, dairy rather than soy promoted cancer growth in these rats.

Another hypothesis suggests that soy might "feminize" men or decrease fertility. The studies do not support this theory. Dr. Neal Barnard, president of the Physicians Committee for Responsible Medicine, states in a 2012 *Huffington Post* article that "the results of human studies clearly show no negative at all on men's hormonal function, testosterone levels, or sperm count." There is no conclusive evidence that soy will reduce a man's fertility.

SOY AND HEART HEALTH

The evidence in regard to soy's effects on heart health is positive, or at least neutral (in smaller amounts). In her article, "Sorting out the Soy Story," Kathleen DesMaisons, one of the "cautiously indifferent" writers on the soy fence, cites two studies that conclude that soy reduces cholesterol and promotes heart health because it "relaxes coronary arteries, reduces inflammation, and reduces blood lipids, homocysteine, and blood pressure." The *New England Journal of Medicine* published one of these studies in 1995. In the article, nearly forty studies were reviewed, most of which indicated that consumption of soy protein instead of animal protein lowered total cholesterol, LDL (bad) cholesterol, and triglycerides. Walter C. Willett, M.D., author of *Eat, Drink, and Be Healthy: The Harvard Medical School Guide to Healthy Eating* claims that these results are not "particularly terrific evidence" that soy promotes positive heart health. Willett states that to "meet the FDA's target for soy—which is half that described in the *New England Journal of Medicine* report—you would need to drink four 8-ounce glasses of soy milk a day...or eat almost a pound of tofu."

This conundrum for consumers is not helped by the evidence. Is soy heart healthy? Yes, according to the studies. Is it heart unhealthy? No, not according to the studies. Could it be neither, at least for those of us who eat it in moderation? Possibly.

When reading the information on soy, I found that many of the studies examined what happens when a person replaces unhealthy proteins—specifically animal proteins—with soy. What this means is that soy, while heart healthy in moderate degrees (and again, at the very least not *bad* for the heart), has these effects on an otherwise healthy diet. While numerous studies indicate that animal protein increases the risk for heart disease and other ailments, the studies on soy- and plant-based diets indicate an associated reduction in risk.

Soy and Allergies

Soy is also a "Top 8" allergen, which means that like dairy, the incidences of allergies to soy is high. Soy contains fifteen proteins that can cause allergic reactions. Soy allergies are most common among children, though studies show that most—60 percent—will outgrow their allergy by age ten. A dairy-free, soy-free child or adult's reliance on other dairy alternatives,

such as almond, coconut, hemp, and rice, is key, and avoidance of processed foods is even more of a necessity, because they include soy-derived and dairy-derived ingredients. As with dairy allergies, subsisting on a primarily whole-foods, plant-based diet is the best way to avoid unwanted allergens in your food.

Soy and GMO Crops

The term "genetically modified organisms" (or GMO) is a buzzword in the anti-soy movement. A genetically modified food is an organic food with changes made to its DNA. By all rights, genetically modified foods are something to buzz about, especially because they are implicated in serious health conditions and rainforest deforestation (one argument is that land for GMO crops is one the key drivers of the disappearance of the Amazon rainforest, and that these GMO products most often go to feed livestock, not humans). "Golden rice," for example, is modified to provide added nutrients to staple crops in developing countries, where nutrient deficiencies have devastating health consequences. More conventional genetically modified foods are modified to be resistant to pesticides, herbicides, and viruses, or to delay ripening.

These luxuries for conventional farmers can create hazards for consumers. According to an article published in 2009 in *Critical Reviews in Food Science and Nutrition*, "the results of most studies with GM [genetically modified] foods indicate that they may cause some common toxic effects such as hepatic, pancreatic, renal, or reproductive effects and may alter the hematological, biochemical, and immunologic parameters." Because GMO crops are herbicide resistant, they may also contain hazardous amounts of pesticides that would hypothetically be ingested by farm animals or humans.

What does this have to do with soy? Soy is second only to corn in its percentage of genetically modified crops. According to the USDA, 93 percent of soybean crops in the United States were genetically modified in 2012. According to a report published by the International Service for the Acquisition of Agri-Biotech Applications in the same year, 81 percent of soybean crops worldwide are genetically modified. An article in *Mother Jones* in the same year details that at least 70 percent of processed foods in the United States contain genetically modified ingredients. Yet, the U.S. government does not, at the time of this writing, require food manufacturers to indicate the presence of GMOs in their products, which means that any processed foods in your pantry may contain GMOs, and possibly GM soy.

What's more disconcerting is that information on the health effects of GMO crops is largely unexplored, at least scientifically. In a review of GMO studies published in the *International Journal of Biological Sciences*, several scientists concluded that to close the health debate on genetically modified products, more thorough and accurate testing should be done, and that those studies previously performed by GMO companies are flawed and inconclusive.

We are told to believe that products with GMO are safe, even when articles proclaim that GM ingredients may be dangerous to our health, cause allergic reactions, or harm the environment. Many health advocates and environmental advocates are staying away from GMO products until there is more of an investigation and more transparency in the GM industry.

So what is the answer? Avoiding processed foods, which may contain any number of GMOs, including genetically modified soy, is the first step to knowing what's in your food. If you choose to enjoy soy products such as soymilks, soybeans, and tofu, look for those labeled organic and

"GMO-free" or "No GMO." Dr. Neil Barnard, M.D., advises in an article published in 2012 in the *Huffington Post* that "GMO soy products are fed to cattle and other animals on a daily basis, so it's meat-eaters who should be concerned."

If you're not clearly pro-soy or anti-soy after reading all of the evidence above, it's because many studies come down on both sides of the debate. Others claim indifference. Like many authors and advocates for good health, I prize moderation in all things. I believe that organic non-GMO soy is a healthy alternative to dairy, and that in moderation it is a beneficial food, especially if replacing a particularly unhealthy food such as dairy or red meat. Balance and variety are important in any diet, and soy, like any food, can

be overconsumed. An easy way to regulate your consumption of soy is to know what's in your food and avoid processed foods. Soy, like dairy, has become inexpensive and mass-produced, and it has found its way into foods you wouldn't expect.

If you are cautious about soy, be assured that soy is not an essential food source, and that there are plenty of other heart-healthy protein sources and dairy alternatives that do not have the same level of controversy. I believe that the pro-soy outweighs the anti-soy evidence, so you'll find some recipes in this book that include soy products. If you are uncomfortable cooking with soy, replace soymilk with any one of the other dairy-free milk options detailed in the book, use soy-free margarine or coconut oil, and skip the tofu.

Soy Products and How to Use Them

Edamame (soybeans) are green soybeans. Rich and buttery tasting, they are most often served as an appetizer or finger food in Japanese cuisine. Edamame can be boiled, steamed, or roasted and then lightly salted for a simple dish. They can be blended into a dip similar to hummus, or added to a salad or rice dish.

Miso, a fermented soybean paste, has been a traditional ingredient in Japanese cooking for centuries. Americans are most familiar with miso soup, but I like to use miso in my dairy-free cheeses to replace the fermented flavor. For examples, try Almond Cheese (page 60), Brazil Nut Cheese (page 59), and Cashew Cheese (page 58).

Soymilk is the precursor to tofu in the same way that milk is the precursor to cheese. Look for organic and non-GMO soymilks, and use soymilk in any recipe that calls for regular milk. Soymilk works well for dairy-free ice cream, puddings, sauces, shakes, smoothies, and soups. If you choose to make your own tofu, you'll start with soymilk, which is made from soybeans and water. To make soymilk at home (page 54), buy non-GMO soybeans. Many soymilks are enriched with calcium, vitamin D, and other nutrients.

Tempeh, a fermented product made of whole soybeans, is most often sold in vacuum-sealed packages. It has a nutty flavor and texture, and although it is not commonly used to replace dairy, vegetarians and vegans often use it to replace meat. Tempeh can be fried or baked for a snack or crumbled into a chili in place of ground meat.

Block or **Chinese-style tofu,** also called bean curd, is made from soymilk and a coagulating agent such as gypsum (also known as calcium sulfate) or mineral salt. Chinese-style tofu is sold in blocks suspended in liquid and classified by its level of "give": medium, medium-firm, firm, and extra-firm. Most of the recipes in this book call for firm or extra-firm tofu, because it can withstand a bit more handling and can be crumbled into curds that resemble cheese (see Tofu Ricotta, page 63). Chinese-style tofu is typically sold in refrigerated sections of large-scale groceries, health food stores, and Asian markets.

Fermented tofu is prepared by fermenting small cubes of tofu in a rice-wine brine and packing them into jars. In the United States, it is usually found in Asian markets, and can also be purchased online. Like most fermented products, fermented tofu is intensely flavored and, well, a little stinky, which is why it works well in dairy-free recipes such as Cashew Blue Cheese (page 62) that need an extra salty, aromatic flavor. Some fermented tofus are brined with sugar, some with chile flakes or spicy chile sauce—but for making cheese substitutes, I stick with white fermented tofu, prepared with only tofu, water, rice wine, and salt.

Silken tofu, like Chinese-style tofu, is made from soymilk and a coagulating agent, but unlike Chinese-style tofu, it is smooth with no visible curds. It's not a good substitute for ricotta cheese, but it is a perfect dairy-free and vegan substitute for cheese sauces like the one in Better Eggplant Parmesan (page 118) and dairy-free custards, puddings, and pie fillings like Chocolate Peanut Butter Pie (page 151). Silken tofu is sold in large-scale groceries, health food stores, and Asian markets in paper or cardboard packaging in both refrigerated and nonrefrigerated sections. Silken tofu, unlike the Chinese style, does not need to be stored in the refrigerator, but at cool or room temperature in a dry place such as a pantry or kitchen cabinet.

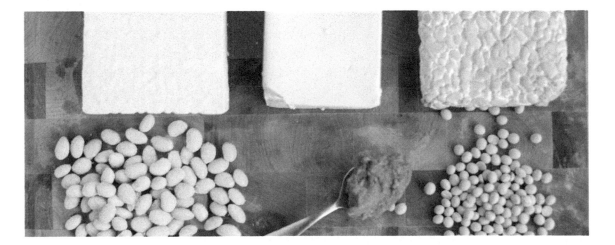

Chapter 5

COCONUT MYTHS AND FACTS

COCONUT IS HANDS-DOWN one of the best substitutes for dairy. Coconut milk is rich and creamy, so it works well in dairy-free cream soups, sauces, smoothies, and desserts. Like cream, a little goes a long way. Coconut milk beverages are sold in cartons next to other alternative milks, and can be used in your morning cereal. These are lower in fat but usually contain sweeteners and additives, so when I mention coconut products and coconut milk in this chapter or in the recipes, I am not referring to the beverages, but to canned or homemade coconut milk. Coconut water is lauded for its natural potassium content, which makes it ideal for quenching post-workout thirst. I use coconut oil in almost any dish as a replacement for butter or oil, and it can even be rubbed into the skin during a massage. I add coconut meat or flakes to cookies, oatmeal, or pie crusts, or serve it as a snack. Coconut butter makes an excellent sandwich spread or addition to dairy-free frostings. All of these coconut products are widely available and, with the exception of coconut oil and coconut butter, inexpensive. Most important, despite what you may have heard elsewhere, coconut is good for you.

Why Coconut Has Such a Bad Rap

There's a reason why coconut was demonized for so long. Coconut is high in saturated fat, and our culture is regularly flogged with the idea that low-fat—and especially low-saturated-fat—foods lead to good health. There is some truth to this, but the source of the fat and what happens after it is sourced can make all the difference when it comes to nutrition. Like almonds, there's more to coconut's fat than might meet the label-reading eye.

An article published in *The New York Times* explored why coconut oil was portrayed as a villain in the past. It cites a study published in 1994 that claimed that a bucket of movie theater popcorn popped in coconut oil contained as much saturated fat as six Big Macs. Studies like this created a stigma against the humble palm fruit. However, the problem with equating coconut oil to six Big Macs, according to Thomas Brenna, professor of nutritional sciences at Cornell University, is that the studies on coconut oil used partially hydrogenated coconut oil, not extra-virgin coconut oil that has not been chemically processed and contains good-for-you ingredients like essential fatty acids and antioxidants.

Partially hydrogenated and hydrogenated fats create trans fats, which, according to the Harvard School of Public Health, increase levels of bad cholesterol (LDL) while decreasing levels of good cholesterol (HDL). Trans fats also promote inflammation, implicated in chronic conditions such as heart disease, stroke, and diabetes. Hydrogenated fats were invented to create products that don't spoil as easily and to turn liquids into solids, which makes transportation easier. In other words, they were created for the processed food industry. Coconut products in their natural form are not the same thing at all.

Can a Food High in Saturated Fat Have Health Benefits?

Pure nonhydrogenated coconut products are still high in saturated fat, and so the confusion between studies performed on coconut products containing trans fats and saturated fats lives on. What is essential in understanding label-reading and good health, however, is how much intervention a whole food undergoes before reaching your plate.

Not all saturated fats are the same in terms of health. They behave differently in the body, because they're made up of different kinds of fatty acids. Fats and oils, both saturated and unsaturated, are made up of chains of small compounds of fatty acids, which come in three sizes: small, medium, and long. These then form triglycerides, which also come in short, medium, or long chains. Most of the fats that we digest, both good and bad, are long-chain varieties.

Coconut oil is unique because it is comprised primarily of medium-chain fatty acids. Medium-chain fatty acids (MCTs) are easier to digest than long-chain varieties, which means that they can more easily be converted into energy. According to Bruce Fife, author of *The Coconut Miracle*, it is one of the reasons that coconut is a healing food, and also why coconut has been used in intravenous solutions for patients in hospitals and in baby formula for decades. He cites studies that suggest that coconut oil may also increase endurance in athletes because of its ability to convert into energy easily.

Some articles have speculated that the medium-chain fatty acids present in coconut oil also aid weight loss, but there is not yet enough evidence to prove this. The reasoning is that because medium-chain triglycerides are more easily converted into energy, they are less likely to be stored as fat and cause weight gain. A study published in 1981 in the *American Journal of Clinical Nutrition* discussed the diets of two groups of Polynesian peoples and found that although the populations' intakes of coconut were high (35 percent and 50 percent of total caloric intake), they were almost completely free of heart diseases and complications and maintained healthy weights.

Beyond the length of its triglycerides, coconut contains individual fatty acids studied for their ability to fight various kinds of infections. About half of coconut's fat is composed of lauric acid, a fatty acid that is associated with antimicrobial and antiviral properties. Mary Enig, Ph.D., a noted U.S. lipid biochemist, has written extensively on coconut oil and particularly lauric acid. She explains in *Coconut: In Support of Good Health in the 21st Century* that lauric acid is converted into monolaurin in the human body, which is then used to destroy lipid-coated viruses such as HIV. In a study published in 2005, researchers found that monolaurin, in combination with herbal essential oils, inhibits pathogenic bacteria in mice and in the lab. Other studies show that capric acid, another fatty acid present in coconut oil, is an antiviral and antibacterial agent that may help prevent sexually transmitted infections and food-borne illness. Medium-chain triglycerides, including lauric acid and capric acid, have antiviral benefits when added to infant formula, as shown in a study published in the *Journal of Nutritional Biochemistry* in 1995.

So coconut oil may do more than just prevent illness—it may actually play a role in treating illness.

Because the arguments against saturated fats are generally related to heart health, I want to tackle this objection last. It's pretty simple—coconut oil, according to the evidence, is not a threat to heart health as we were led to believe in the 1990s. Studies like one published in 2004 in *Clinical Biochemistry* show that virgin coconut oil actually increases good HDL cholesterol while simultaneously decreasing bad LDL cholesterol. (Dairy, as mentioned earlier, and especially butter, increases LDL cholesterol, according to studies.) In other words, coconut is good for you, saturated fat and all.

Coconut Products and How to Use Them

Coconut oil has a sweet, fragrant taste that shines in savory dishes and sweet pastries alike. It is the most similar plant-based oil to butter. It stays solid when cold, softens at room temperature, and turns to liquid when heated. It has a mellow presence, like butter, so it doesn't overpower other ingredients but highlights them. Extra-virgin coconut oil is expensive—there is no getting around it. But you get what you pay for. Because I use coconut oil in so many dishes and often spread it on my morning toast, I generally buy a large tub of it at a wholesale store to save a few bucks.

Coconut butter combines coconut oil and the coconut meat, so it's thick, is high in fiber, and spreads like peanut butter. You shouldn't use it in place of butter or oil in a recipe, but I've found it works well in dairy-free frostings and cookies. Making your own coconut butter is easy, too, and will save you a bundle. Just take a bag or two of unsweetened shredded coconut and place it in a high-powered blender for about 5 minutes, stopping the blender to scrape down the sides periodically, until the butter is thick and creamy.

Coconut milk is rich, nutty, and flavorful, so I prefer to use it in dishes that are meant to have a coconut flavor. Creamy pureed soups, nutty dairy-free cheeses, curry sauces, and morning oatmeal are great dishes for coconut. Coconut milk is sold in large grocery stores and health food stores in cans, cartons, and packages—and in the freezer aisle of some specialty markets. (As mentioned earlier, coconut milk beverages found in cartons in the dairy case are not the same as whole coconut milk, and cannot be substituted in recipes because they contain watered-down coconut milk with sugars and other additives. I stick to canned or frozen coconut milk.)

Although coconut milk is widely available and relatively inexpensive, making your own coconut milk at home is fun and less expensive than buying it in a can. Try Raw Coconut Milk (page 50) and Better-Than-Canned Coconut Milk (page 52) in your next soup or cup of hot cocoa for a treat.

Coconut cream is really coconut milk with less water. Recipes that call for coconut cream advise you to chill your can of full-fat coconut milk overnight, puncture the can and drain out the water, then open the can and remove the thick white creamy part. This is your coconut cream, and it can be used in a variety of recipes, including the Coconut Crème Brûlée (page 152).

Chapter 6

RICE, THE ALLERGY-FRIENDLY OPTION

DAIRY, SOY, TREE NUTS, and wheat are all on the list of the world's most allergenic foods. Rice, the most hypoallergenic substitute, often becomes the stand-in in alternative diets. Sweeter and lighter than other milk alternatives, rice milk has a pleasant taste and refreshing texture, and makes a great "starter" milk for people new to dealing with allergies. Rice-based dairy-free products are widely available in markets, are low in fat, and offer many nutrients. Rice milk is also simple and inexpensive to make without artificial flavors and additives.

Rice—at least in its whole-food form—is good for you, too. Often viewed as a nutritional lightweight or a complex carbohydrate without much else to offer, this humble grain has more to offer than you might realize, including a bit of controversy.

Most commercial rice milks use brown rice as a base, but many recipes for homemade rice milk call for white rice. Just as understanding the differences between fats is important, so is understanding the differences between rice varieties. Not surprisingly, making your own rice milk is your best bet.

How Brown and White Rice Compare

In the West, we primarily deal with two colors of rice: brown rice and white rice. Using brown or white rice makes major differences in nutrition and in cooking. White rice cooks quickly, is inexpensive, and has a soft texture and sweet undertone once prepared, but due to processing, it doesn't offer us much more than calories. Brown rice has a nutty flavor, rich texture, longer cooking time, and shorter shelf life, which makes it more expensive but nutritionally more valuable.

Brown rice is essentially unprocessed rice—the only part that has been removed from brown rice is the hull. White rice, also referred to as "polished" rice, lacks the hull, bran layers, and germ, so most of the essential nutrients and fiber are gone. These essential nutrients include B vitamins, calcium, magnesium, and selenium, all health-promoting agents important to a dairy-free diet. The B vitamins found in brown rice (B_1, B_3, and B_6) maintain proper circulation, nervous system health, and healthy skin. Calcium and magnesium are essential to bone health and numerous bodily functions, and the mineral selenium is associated with the prevention of free radicals, cancer prevention, and heart health. The change in the physical composition of rice that occurs during processing has several health implications, namely that eating brown rice is good for us, while white rice is only just better than junk food.

Removing the bran and germ from the rice during polishing means that people who consume white rice miss out on most, if not all, of rice's nutritional benefits, including all of the nutrients listed above as well as other health-protective properties. Brown rice contains about 4 g of fiber per cup (165 g) of cooked rice. Having more fiber in your diet is consistently associated with less disease and specifically heart disease in numerous studies, including expansive studies like the Nurses' Health Study. However, there are more health-boosting components in brown rice than just the fiber alone. The results of a study conducted by researchers at the Cardiovascular Research Center and Department of Physiology at Temple University School of Medicine suggest that a component in rice's tissue layer that is stripped away when processed may protect against high blood pressure and atherosclerosis by naturally blocking the endocrine protein that triggers both of these conditions. Another study published in the *American Journal of Clinical Nutrition* showed that rice bran oil actually lowers cholesterol, even more so than defatted rice bran. What this means is that if companies remove the bran for the fiber but leave out rice's lipid component (bran oil), you'll miss out on the cholesterol-lowering effects and heart-protective properties of the rice.

Like most processed foods, white rice provides fewer health benefits than its whole-food counterpart, and there are added risks associated with its consumption, such as an increased risk for developing type 2 diabetes. A study published in the *British Medical Journal* in 2012 found that participants in the study who had a higher consumption of white rice were 27 percent more likely to develop diabetes. The researchers admit that it's difficult to blame white rice entirely for this spike—it could be the combination of an otherwise unhealthy lifestyle with the addition of white rice, which has a high score on the glycemic index. But because foods with high glycemic index scores are associated with a higher risk for developing type 2 diabetes, the findings are noteworthy. Another study performed by the Department of Nutrition at the Harvard School of Public Health likewise found that substituting brown rice for white rice may lower risk for type 2 diabetes, which could be related to any one of brown rice's nutritional properties—fiber content, bran oil, vitamins and minerals, or some other component we have yet to discover. So stick with brown rice—bran oil and all. It prevents illness and disease, while white rice and dairy products contribute to illness and disease.

Rice, Arsenic, and What to Know

Even whole foods can be less healthy if grown in a toxic environment. In 2012, findings published by *Consumer Reports* went viral, claiming that rice and rice-based products contain arsenic, a naturally occurring element that has carcinogenic and lethal properties at high doses. The researchers found varying levels of arsenic in a variety of rice-based products, including infant formulas and cereals as well as in white but especially brown rice.

The EPA has no listed safe levels of arsenic consumption, so this further complicates the situation. If there is no safe amount, shouldn't we avoid all foods that we know contain arsenic? What the researchers recommend is a more moderate approach, including eating a varied diet, cooking with a variety of grains, thoroughly washing rice before using, and cooking rice using a 6 to 1 ratio of water to rice. Cooks know that this much water results in a mushy rice product. What I do to remedy this is cook my brown rice the same way I do for Brown Rice Milk (page 56), which is to keep it at a low boil for the duration of cooking, then cover and place off the heat to steam for 10 minutes or so. Researchers also recommend having your home water tested for arsenic levels if you're concerned, which you can do by calling a local certified lab.

According to *Consumer Reports*, the arsenic contamination is a result of farming practices in the United States. The United States is the world's leading consumer of arsenic, using about 1.6 million tons of arsenic since 1910. Lead-arsenate insecticides were banned decades ago, but their residues still linger in U.S. soil today, and arsenical ingredients are still permitted in animal feed and transferred into the soil through manure. There are hopes to reduce the amount of arsenic still in use today and, therefore, prevent further exposure.

The rice industry, meanwhile, is protecting its interests. The USA Rice Federation's statement on arsenic contamination of rice argues that the people of the United States should trust the FDA's monitoring of our foods, that "arsenic is an element that is naturally present in the environment in soil, water, air, and food," that "humans have been exposed to trace levels of it in their foods for thousands of years," and that "assertions about high levels of arsenic in U.S. rice are not new, nor are they accurate."

There is, of course, a middle ground, and it is one of reasonable caution and moderation. Dr. Gary Ginsberg, noted toxicologist, published an article in the *Huffington Post* the month following the release of the *Consumer Reports* findings. He explained that the knowledge that rice is good at absorbing arsenic and other toxins from soil and irrigation is not new, and has been evident in studies for decades. He advises that although the latest report was one of the most extensive, consumers still should maintain perspective. "The FDA sampled a variety of rice products and found 1 to 10 g per serving across the range of brown, white, basmati, rice cereal and rice cakes," he says. "For an adult eating a few servings a week, this amount is well below what current drinking water standards allow ... but one needs to consider all sources of exposure and until the FDA review is out, moderation would be wise."

As far as milk alternatives go, rice is a hypo-allergenic solution for many who cannot consume multiple allergenic foods. If consumed in its whole-foods form as brown rice, it is a functional food with many nutritional benefits. In light of the recent reports regarding the elevated levels of arsenic in brown rice, it is best to consume brown rice as part of a moderate, varied diet, and to thoroughly wash rice before cooking or using in recipes such as Brown Rice Milk (page 56). Brown rice has excellent health benefits if grown, harvested, and prepared properly, so research where your brown rice comes from.

It is easy to focus on one aspect of food and decide that the food itself is either good or bad, especially in the face of scary information such as arsenic contamination. For example, brown-rice-based milks are readily available, but as with those cartons of coconut milk, their labels indicate artificial flavors and sweeteners. Rice milk made at home has a naturally sweet flavor that doesn't require a lot of added sweeteners, and I find that store-bought varieties taste like candy. A food is only as good as the sum of its parts, as is a diet. A healthy, varied diet of whole foods is your best protection against disease, illness, and contamination.

Chapter 7

HEMP: ANCIENT CROP, MODERN MILK

HEMP SEED, another nutritionally functional food, is an ancient crop that has been used in countries such as China for thousands of years as an antibiotic, digestive, and diuretic. Fabrics such as rope, sails on cargo ships, and canvas have been made from hemp for centuries. Abraham Lincoln allegedly used hemp oil in his oil lamp. Most recently, hemp has been marketed as a health food in the West, as well as a soy-free substitute for dairy. Like almond milk and cashew milk, hemp seeds can be blended with water and then strained through a cheesecloth to make hemp milk at home, to be used in place of milk in countless recipes. Hemp seed butter is found in large grocers and specialty health food stores alike, and it makes an excellent spread on toast and substitute for peanut butter.

Although hemp seed is a derivative of the plant *Cannabis Sativa,* it will not get you high. However, because it is part of the plant, as of this writing it is not legal to cultivate hemp seed in the United States, which means that hemp seeds sold in the United States come from elsewhere. This makes hemp seed pricey, but expense is really its only downside. Current regulations in the United States have hampered research on hemp seed, but the research that's been obtained thus far is overwhelmingly positive and points to hemp as a superfood that we, in the West, are just beginning to understand.

Benefits of Hemp

As discussed previously, fat—and specifically the kind of fat in foods—is highly significant when it comes to health. Most of the beneficial nutrients obtained from almonds, coconut, and even brown rice are found in the respective food's natural, healthy fats. Hemp is no different. One of hemp's primary nutritional benefits is that hemp seed oil contains an almost perfect balance of omega-6 and omega-3 fatty acids. According to Jonny Bowden, Ph.D., author of *The 150 Healthiest Foods on Earth*, as well as many other authors on fats and health, hemp seed has the best ratio of these essential fatty acids of all oils. This balance is important to healthy bodily function. The U.S. diet has an overabundance of omega-6 (and refined, poor-quality omega-6) and not enough omega-3. An imbalance either way, however, is detrimental to good health (too much omega-3 can be problematic also), which is why hemp's balance of the two is so beneficial. Omega-6 fatty acids are associated with healthier hearts, as evidenced by a research paper published by the American Heart Association. It found that the consumption of 5 to 10 percent of energy from omega-6 fatty acids decreases the risk of coronary heart disease. In other words, the healthy fats in hemp may prevent some of the diseases that dairy fats are associated with causing.

Omega-3 fatty acids are important for many functions within the body as well, including heart health, brain health, and behavioral health. An article published in *The American Journal for Clinical Nutrition* reviewed thirty-eight scholarly articles and concluded that omega-3 fatty acids may prevent coronary heart disease; stroke; essential fatty acid deficiency in infancy, which leads to improper retinal and brain development; autoimmune disorders; Crohn's disease; cancer (breast, colon, and prostate); hypertension; and arthritis.

Hemp seed is also rich in a particular polyunsaturated fatty acid that is difficult to find in a Western diet: gamma-linolenic acid (known as GLA), which can inhibit inflammatory responses in the body and therefore prevent disease. (An article published in 2012 in the *Wall Street Journal* examined recent research from scientists that indicates that heart disease, diabetes, Alzheimer's, stroke, and cancer are all linked to chronic inflammation.) In a randomized, double-blind crossover trial conducted in 2006, two groups of participants consumed either flaxseed oil (one of the best natural sources of omega-3) or hemp seed oil. The hemp seed group experienced an increase in GLA, while the flaxseed oil group did not. Participants in the hemp seed group also had a lower total-cholesterol to HDL-cholesterol ratio than the flaxseed oil group.

Hemp seeds also contain protein—about 5 g per 2 tablespoons (16 g)—as well as fiber, vitamin E, phosphorous, potassium, sodium, magnesium, calcium, iron, zinc, and all essential amino acids including the amino acid arginine, which has been shown in studies like the Third National Health Nutrition and Examination Survey to reduce the risk of cardiovascular disease.

Although researchers agree that more clinical studies and specifically human studies should be conducted on hemp seed's nutritional properties and health benefits, the majority of evidence weighs in favor of the plant everyone likes to regulate. Hemp's fat composition, vitamin and mineral content, and fiber all make it a candidate for a superbly healthy food.

Taste Considerations and How to Use Hemp

Hemp seeds and hemp seed oil are nutty and earthy in flavor, similar in taste to sunflower seeds and sunflower oil, but with a little extra bite. Hemp seed is great eaten in its whole hulled form as a snack, sprinkled on a salad, or made into hemp milk, a luscious, healthy substitute to dairy enjoyed on its own or used in preparing any of the dairy-free ice creams, milkshakes, puddings, and other creamy dishes in this book. Spread hemp seed butter on toast or instead of peanut butter on a sandwich. Try hemp seed oil in salad dressings, drizzled over veggies, or added to smoothies, but don't heat it, because the omega-3 fatty acids present in hemp are highly unstable at high temperatures and release toxic by-products. As a result, hemp seeds and hemp seed oil turn rancid fairly quickly, so both require a little extra care in storing. To prevent rancidity, store hemp seed oil and hemp seeds in dark containers in cool, dry places such as the refrigerator, and do not use either past the producers' expiration date. Above all, let your senses guide you—you'll know if a product is rancid by its smell and taste. Hemp oil has a pungent stench once rancid, and will no longer taste earthy and nutty but will be sour, bitter, or just unpleasant.

As more studies come out on hemp seed and the bans and regulations are lifted in the United States, hemp may become more accessible and cultivated locally. If so, this could extend the shelf life of hemp products and prevent early rancidity by reducing transit times.

Chapter 8

MAKING DAIRY-FREE MILKS, BUTTER, CHEESES, AND YOGURTS

KNOWING WHAT IS IN your food is important to both a dairy-free diet and a healthy one, and there's no better way to find out than to make it yourself. Fortunately, making your own dairy-free products—additive free, added sugar free—at home is easy and generally less expensive than buying them in a store.

This chapter explores some of my favorite homemade milk substitutes, dairy-free yogurt recipes, nut-based cheese recipes, and other homemade substitutes for dairy, all prepared with healthier options such as coconut, nuts, heart-healthy oils, and soy. Stock up on some cheesecloth, take out the blender, and get started.

Almond Milk

Making Almond Milk at home is simple and relatively inexpensive, and it allows you to know exactly what's in your glass. Flavor your almond milk however it suits you: agave, honey, and even a dash of cinnamon or cocoa powder can create a whole new taste.

YIELD: 10 CUPS (2.4 L)

2 cups (290 g) raw almonds
Cold water, for soaking
8 cups (1.9 L) cold water
3 tablespoons (60 g) maple syrup (optional)
1 teaspoon fresh-squeezed lemon juice
¼ teaspoon sea salt, plus more to taste

① **Soak the almonds.** Place the almonds in a bowl just big enough for them and fill with water to cover. Cover the container and soak the almonds overnight. Drain the almonds the following day and discard the soaking water.

② **Blend with water.** Place almonds, 8 cups (1.9 L) water, maple syrup (if using), lemon juice, and sea salt in a blender. Blend until smooth, with only small grains throughout.

③ **Strain.** Line a large bowl with cheesecloth, leaving some hanging over the edge. Pour the liquid slowly into the cheesecloth-lined bowl, then gather up the sides of the cloth, creating a sack. Squeeze out the milk into the bowl until only solids remain in the cheesecloth. Discard the solids and transfer the milk into a pitcher or covered container and store in the refrigerator. Homemade Almond Milk will settle and separate—this is normal. Stir before serving to recombine. Almond Milk will keep in an airtight container in the refrigerator for 3–4 days.

Raw Coconut Milk

Cracking the coconut is the most difficult part of making your own Raw Coconut Milk; after you've opened your coconut, you're almost there.

YIELD: 5-7 CUPS (1.2-1.7 L), DEPENDING ON COCONUT SIZE

1 medium coconut
3-4 cups (0.7-1 L) water
Pinch of salt
Agave or maple syrup (optional)

(1) **Open the coconut.** Find the "equator" line that runs completely around the coconut—it is a line physically indented in the coconut that wraps around the coconut's widest part. (If you don't see an equator line, just whack around the widest part of the coconut with a hammer or the blunt edge of a heavy knife, and one will quickly appear.) Use the blunt edge of a heavy knife, or alternatively a hammer, and whack the coconut along the equatorial line, turning the coconut as you go, until you've turned the coconut 3 or 4 times. The coconut will split in half. Catch the juice in a bowl.

(2) **Scoop out the flesh.** Break the coconut into smaller pieces to make it easier to remove the flesh. Use a fork, grapefruit spoon, or other utensil to help you dislodge the meat from the shell. Rind will stay attached to the meat, but don't worry—it's edible and will be strained from the milk.

(3) **Blend with water.** Place the pieces of coconut meat and the juice in a blender. Fill the blender with water just about 2-3 inches (5-8 cm) over the coconut. Every coconut is different, but usually it comes out to 3-4 cups (0.7-1 L) of added water. Add the salt. Blend until smooth, with only small grains throughout.

(4) **Strain.** Line a large bowl with cheesecloth, leaving some hanging over the edge. Pour the liquid slowly into the cheesecloth-lined bowl, then gather up the sides, creating a sack. Squeeze out the milk into the bowl until only solids remain in the cheesecloth. Discard the solids, transfer the milk into a pitcher or covered container, and store in the refrigerator. Stir before serving to recombine. Add optional ingredients to sweeten, if desired. Raw Coconut Milk will keep in an airtight container in the refrigerator for 3-4 days.

Better-Than-Canned Coconut Milk

For coconut milk similar to canned, try this method. The result is smoother and thicker than raw coconut milk. It's also a bit easier on the hands than making raw coconut milk. The meat is much easier to remove after baking it in the oven.

YIELD: 5–7 CUPS (1.2–1.7 L), DEPENDING ON COCONUT SIZE

1 medium coconut
3–4 cups (0.7–1 L) water
Pinch of salt
Agave or maple syrup (optional)

① **Open the coconut.** Find the "equator" line that runs completely around the coconut—it is a line indented in the coconut that wraps around the coconut's widest part. (If you don't see an equator line, just whack around the widest part of the coconut with a hammer or the blunt edge of a heavy knife, and one will quickly appear.) Use the blunt edge of a very heavy knife or, alternatively, a hammer, and whack the coconut along the equatorial line, turning the coconut as you go, until you've turned the coconut 3 or 4 times. The coconut will split in half. Be sure to catch the juice in a bowl and set this aside. Reserve the juice.

② **Bake, then remove the meat.** Preheat the oven to 375° F (190° C, or gas mark 5). Wrap the coconut halves completely in foil. Bake for 45 minutes to 1 hour. Remove the halves and cool for 5–10 minutes. Using your hands or a fork, ease or pry the meat away from the shell to remove.

③ **Blend with water.** Place the pieces of coconut meat and the reserved juice in a blender. Fill the blender with water 2–3 inches (5–8 cm) over the coconut. Every coconut is different, but usually it comes out to 3–4 cups (0.7–1 L) of added water. Add the salt. Blend until smooth, with only small grains throughout.

④ **Strain.** Line a large bowl with cheesecloth, leaving some hanging over the edge. Pour the liquid slowly into the cheesecloth-lined bowl, then gather up the sides, creating a sack. Squeeze out the milk into the bowl until only solids remain in the cheesecloth. Discard the solids, transfer the milk into a pitcher or covered container, and store in the refrigerator. Stir before serving to recombine. Add optional ingredients to taste, if desired. Use in soups, sauces, and desserts. Better-Than-Canned Coconut Milk will keep in an airtight container in the refrigerator for 3–4 days.

Cashew Milk

Cashews have a naturally buttery taste that results in a delicious, smooth milk. Use Cashew Milk in any recipes that call for milk, or enjoy it straight from the glass.

YIELD: 8-10 CUPS (1.9-2.4 L)

2 cups (270 g) raw cashews

Cold water, for soaking

8 cups (1.9 L) water

Sea salt

Agave nectar or maple syrup (optional)

1. **Soak the cashews.** Place the cashews in a bowl just big enough for them, and fill the container with water to just cover the cashews. Cover the container and soak the cashews overnight. Drain the cashews the following day and discard the soaking water.

2. **Blend with water.** Place cashews and the 8 cups (1.9 L) of water in a blender. Blend until smooth, with only small grains throughout.

3. **Strain.** Line a large bowl with cheesecloth, leaving some hanging over the edge. Pour the liquid slowly into the cheesecloth-lined bowl, then gather up the sides of the cloth, creating a sack. Squeeze out the milk into the bowl until only solids remain in the cheesecloth. Discard the solids and transfer the milk into a pitcher or covered container and store in the refrigerator. Homemade cashew milk will settle and separate—this is normal. Stir before serving to recombine and add salt and optional sweeteners to taste. Cashew Milk will keep in an airtight container in the refrigerator for 3-4 days.

Soymilk

This milk is one of the least expensive to make, second only to brown rice milk. It requires no special equipment, either—just a little soaking time, a little boiling, and a little draining. Typically, I use agave or maple syrup as a sweetener for alternative milks, but for rice milk, I like cane sugar best. Feel free to experiment with sweeteners and flavorings until you find the ones that work best for you.

YIELD: 8-9 CUPS (1.9-2.1 L)

3 cups (750 g) organic non-GMO dried soybeans, rinsed well

Cold water, for soaking

10½ cups (2.5 L) water

⅛ teaspoon sea salt

¼ cup (50 g) organic cane sugar or liquid sweetener

① **Soak the soybeans.** Place the soybeans in a large pot or bowl. Pour 7-8 cups (1.7-1.9 L) cold water over the beans. Cover the container and soak the soybeans overnight. Drain the beans the following day and discard the soaking liquid.

② **Blend with water and heat.** Place the beans in a blender with the 10½ cups (2.5 L) water and the salt and blend until smooth. (If your blender cannot accommodate this amount, work in two batches.) Transfer to a large pot and place over high heat. Bring the milk to a low boil, turn down the heat, and simmer for 15 to 20 minutes; scoop any foam that forms on the surface with a wooden spoon or small sieve and discard.

③ **Strain.** Line a large sieve with cheesecloth and place it over a large bowl. Pour the soymilk into the cheesecloth and let it set for about 20 minutes, or until it is cool enough to touch. Gather up the sides of the cheesecloth, and press out any excess liquid. Add optional sweeteners to taste. Store Soymilk in an airtight container in the refrigerator for up to 1 week and use in any dish that calls for dairy.

GOOD USES FOR SOY PULP

The beany, fibrous pulp that you're left with after straining out your soymilk is called *okara*, and it can be used in a variety of recipes, including veggie burgers, vegan meatballs, and traditional Japanese dishes like *unohana*, where it is stir-fried with carrots and soy sauce. It's highly perishable, so use it within a day or two or freeze for a future culinary adventure. Several blogs and websites explore ways to cook the pulp, such as The Okara Project and The Messy Vegetarian.

Brown Rice Milk

This lightly sweet dairy-free milk is the thinnest in consistency of all the alternative milks. It's great for beverages, in baking, and over cereal.

YIELD: 6 CUPS (1.4 L)

10½ cups (2.5 L) water, divided

1 cup (190 g) brown rice, rinsed very well in cold water

½ teaspoon vanilla extract

Salt

Agave nectar or maple syrup (optional)

1. **Cook the rice.** Bring 6 cups (1.4 L) of the water in a large pot to a boil. Add the rice, and stir once to combine. Turn down the heat to medium-high, and cook the rice uncovered at a boil for 30 minutes, stirring occasionally. Carefully pour the rice into a strainer to drain the liquid, giving the strainer a good shake to remove excess water. Return the rice to the pot, cover, and let it rest for 10 minutes.

2. **Blend with water.** Place the rice in a blender with the remaining 4½ cups (1 L) water and vanilla. Blend until smooth, with only small grains throughout.

3. **Strain.** Line a large sieve with cheesecloth and place it over a large bowl. Pour the rice milk into the cheesecloth and let it set for about 20 minutes, or until it is cool enough to touch. Gather up the sides of the cheesecloth and press out any excess liquid. Add salt and sweetener to taste and store in an airtight container in the refrigerator for up to 1 week.

Cashew Sour Cream

Soured with lemon and cider vinegar, this easy-to-make sour cream substitute can be used in any recipe that calls for sour cream.

YIELD: ABOUT 1½ CUPS (345 ML)

2 cups (270 g) raw cashews
Cold water, for soaking
½–¾ teaspoon sea salt
2 teaspoons (10 mL) cider vinegar
Juice of 2 lemons
¼ cup (60 mL) water

1. **Soak the cashews overnight.** Place the cashews in a bowl just big enough for them, and fill with water to just cover the cashews. Cover the container and soak the cashews overnight. Drain the cashews the following day and discard the soaking water.

2. **Blend.** Place the cashews in a blender along with the sea salt, cider vinegar, lemon juice, and ¼ cup (60 mL) water. Blend until creamy and smooth. Refrigerate until chilled. Serve cold. Store in the refrigerator in an airtight container for up to 4 days.

Coconut Sour Cream

This no-blender, no-cook sour cream alternative is rich and delicious and looks like the real deal.

YIELD: ABOUT 2 CUPS (460 ML)

Two 15-ounce (0.4 kg) cans full-fat coconut milk, refrigerated overnight
1 tablespoon (15 mL) lemon juice, plus more to taste
Pinch of sea salt

1. **Make the cream.** Puncture the coconut cans and drain the liquid. Scoop the coconut cream into a small bowl, and mix in the lemon juice and sea salt. Use immediately or store in the refrigerator in an airtight container for up to 2 days.

Cashew Cheese

This dairy-free cheese wheel is so good you'll find it hard to believe that it isn't actually cheese. Nutritional yeast, miso, and lemon juice contribute to its cheesy flavor and appearance; and cashews, coconut milk, almond milk, and agar flakes make up its sliceable, rich texture. Slice and serve with crackers, layer it in a sandwich, or add it to a dairy-free quiche or casserole.

YIELD: ONE 7- TO 8-INCH (18–20 CM) CHEESE WHEEL

2 heaping cups (270 g) raw cashews

½ cup (60 g) nutritional yeast

1 teaspoon salt

2 cups (0.5 L) full-fat coconut milk

1½ cups (0.4 L) unsweetened almond milk

½ cup (40 g) agar flakes (one 1-ounce [28 g] package)

½ cup (120 mL) canola oil or coconut oil

¼ cup (62.5 g) white miso

2 tablespoons (30 mL) fresh lemon juice

① **Grind the cashews.** Place the cashews in a high-quality blender or food processor, and process until very finely ground, stopping the blender or food processor and scraping down the sides occasionally. Add the nutritional yeast and salt, and pulse a few times to incorporate.

② **Make the cheese.** Combine the milks, agar flakes, and oil in a medium saucepan and place over medium-high heat. Stirring constantly, bring the mixture to a simmer, then reduce the heat to medium. Continue stirring often for about 10 minutes until the mixture thickens slightly. It will start off looking "separated," with the oil floating to the top and the agar flakes visible, but should become relatively consistent throughout after cooking. Remove from the heat.

③ **Blend.** Pour the mixture into the blender or food processor. Process with the ground cashews until well blended. Add the miso and fresh lemon juice and blend until smooth.

④ **Chill overnight.** Line a round glass storage bowl (a 7–8-cup [1.5–2 L] storage bowl works well) with plastic wrap, leaving about 2 inches (5 cm) of overhang. Press the plastic wrap so that it adheres to the sides as much as possible. Pour the cheese into the container, cover, and refrigerate overnight or until set. When you're ready to serve, simply lift the cheese out of the container by the plastic and invert it onto a cutting board or serving plate. Cashew Cheese will keep in the refrigerator for 1 week in an airtight container. Serve cold.

Brazil Nut Cheese

Brazil nuts and macadamia nuts combine with coconut oil in this lovely soft and creamy cheese. Spread on sandwiches, serve with crackers and fruit, or add to recipes such as Dairy-Free Quiche Lorraine (page 84).

YIELD: ONE 7- TO 8-INCH (18–20 CM) CHEESE WHEEL

2 cups (270 g) raw Brazil nuts

½ cup (67.5 g) raw macadamia nuts

⅔ cup (80 g) nutritional yeast

1 teaspoon salt

2 cups (0.5 L) full-fat coconut milk

1½ cups (0.4 mL) unsweetened almond milk

½ cup (40 g) agar flakes (one 1-ounce [28 g] package)

½ cup (120 mL) coconut oil

¼ cup (62.5 g) white miso

2 tablespoons (30 mL) fresh lemon juice

① **Grind the nuts.** Place the Brazil nuts and macadamia nuts in a high-quality blender or food processor, and process until very finely ground, stopping the blender or food processor and scraping down the sides occasionally. Add the nutritional yeast and salt, and pulse a few times to incorporate.

② **Make the cheese.** Combine the milks, agar flakes, and oil in a medium saucepan and place over medium-high heat. Stirring constantly, bring the mixture to a simmer, then turn down the heat to medium. Continue stirring often for about 10 minutes until the mixture thickens slightly. It will start off looking separated, with the oil floating to the top and the agar flakes very visible, but it should become relatively consistent throughout after cooking. Remove from the heat.

③ **Blend.** Pour the milk-agar mixture into the blender or food processor. Process with the ground nuts until well blended. Add the miso and fresh lemon juice and blend until smooth.

④ **Chill.** Line a round glass storage container (a 7-8-cup [1.5-2 L] storage bowl works well) with plastic wrap, leaving about 2 inches (5 cm) of overhang. Press the plastic wrap so that it adheres to the sides as much as possible. Pour the cheese into the container, cover, and chill overnight. When you're ready to serve, simply lift the cheese out of the container by the plastic and invert it onto a cutting board or serving plate. Brazil Nut Cheese will keep in the refrigerator for 1 week in an airtight container. Serve cold.

Almond Cheese

This cheese has a pleasantly nutty flavor. Flakes of almond give it a lovely texture and color. Almonds, even soaked, are tough to grind in an everyday blender, so if this is what you have, expect to grind your almonds for a bit longer and to have a slightly more textured cheese. An alternative is to peel the skins off of the almonds before blending. It will take some time, but is not difficult. Simply pinch the skins together with your fingers and remove. Serve Almond Cheese as an appetizer or snack or use in recipes like Baked Mac n' Cheese (page 116).

YIELD: ONE 7- TO 8-INCH (18-20 CM) CHEESE WHEEL

2 cups (290 g) raw almonds

Cold water, for soaking

⅔ cup (80 g) nutritional yeast

1 teaspoon salt

One 15-ounce (440 mL) can full-fat coconut milk

2 cups (0.5 L) almond milk

½ cup (40 g) agar flakes (one 1-ounce [28 g] package)

½ cup (120 mL) extra-virgin olive oil

¼ cup (62.5 g) white miso

2 tablespoons (30 mL) fresh lemon juice

(1) **Soak the almonds.** Place the almonds in a bowl just big enough to fit, and fill with water to just cover the almonds. Cover the container and soak the cashews overnight. Drain the almonds the following day and discard the soaking water.

(2) **Grind.** Place the almonds in a high-quality blender or food processor and process until very finely ground, stopping the blender or food processor and scraping down the sides occasionally. Add the nutritional yeast and salt, and pulse a few times to incorporate. Set aside.

(3) **Make the cheese.** Combine the milks, agar flakes, and oil in a medium saucepan and place over medium-high heat. Stirring constantly, bring the mixture to a simmer, then turn down the heat to medium. Continue stirring often for about 10 minutes until the mixture thickens slightly. It will start off looking "separated," with the oil floating to the top and the agar flakes visible, but should become relatively consistent throughout after cooking. Remove from the heat.

(4) **Blend.** Pour the mixture into the blender or food processor. Process with the ground almonds until well blended. Add the miso and fresh lemon juice and blend until smooth.

(5) **Chill.** Line a round glass storage container (a 7-8-cup [1.5 to 2 L] storage bowl works well) with plastic wrap, leaving about 2 inches (5 cm) of overhang. Press the plastic wrap so that it adheres to the sides. Pour the cheese into the container, cover, and chill overnight. When you're ready to serve, simply lift the cheese out of the container by the plastic and invert it onto a cutting board or serving plate. Almond Cheese will keep in the refrigerator for 1 week in an airtight container. Serve cold.

Cashew Blue Cheese

Fermented tofu and blue algae powder give this cashew cheese its blue swirls and extra cheesy taste. Fermented tofu can be found at Asian markets and blue algae powder at most health stores and online.

YIELD: ONE 7- TO 8-INCH (18–20 CM) CHEESE WHEEL

2 heaping cups (270 g) raw cashews

2 tablespoons (15 g) nutritional yeast

1 teaspoon salt

2 cups (0.5 L) full-fat coconut milk

1½ cups (0.4 L) unsweetened almond milk or soymilk

½ cup (40 g) agar flakes (one 1-ounce [28 g] package)

½ cup (120 mL) canola oil

¼ cup (62.5 mL) white miso

2 tablespoons (30 mL) fresh lemon juice

One 14-ounce (396 g) jar fermented tofu, drained

1 tablespoon (15 g) blue algae powder

① **Grind the cashews.** Place the cashews in a high-quality blender or food processor and process until very finely ground, stopping the blender or food processor and scraping down the sides occasionally. Add the nutritional yeast and salt, and pulse a few times to incorporate. Set aside.

② **Make the cheese.** Combine the milks, agar flakes, and oil. Place in a medium saucepan over medium-high heat. Stirring constantly, bring the mixture to a simmer, then turn down the heat to medium. Continue stirring often for about 10 minutes until the mixture thickens slightly. It will start off looking separated, with the oil floating to the top and the agar flakes very visible, but should become relatively consistent throughout after cooking. Remove from the heat.

③ **Blend.** Pour the milk–agar mixture into the blender or food processor. Process with the cashews until well blended. Add the miso and fresh lemon juice and blend until smooth.

④ **Add the blue.** Place the fermented tofu in a small bowl. Add the blue algae powder and mash very well. Line a round glass storage bowl with plastic wrap, leaving about 2 inches (5 cm) of overhang. Press the plastic wrap so that it adheres to the sides as much as possible. Place a few tablespoons of the blue algae mixture in the bottom of the dish, then pour about one-third of the cashew cheese over this. Add a few more tablespoons of the blue mixture to the cashew cheese, using a spoon to swirl some of the blue into the cashew cheese. Add another third of the cashew cheese, followed by a few more tablespoons of the blue algae mixture (swirling again), followed by the remaining cashew cheese and blue algae mixture.

⑤ **Cover and chill.** Cover the container and chill overnight. When you're ready to serve, simply lift the cheese out of the container by the plastic and invert it onto a cutting board or serving plate. Cashew Blue Cheese will keep in the refrigerator for 1 week in an airtight container. Serve cold.

Cashew Cream Cheese

The longer you strain your Cashew Cream Cheese, the firmer it will become, so don't rush the process—just keep an eye on it and wait until it reaches the consistency you desire.

YIELD: ABOUT 1 CUP (230 G)

1½ cups (200 g) raw cashew pieces
Cold water, for soaking
2 tablespoons (30 mL) fresh lemon juice
3 tablespoons (45 mL) water

1. **Soak the cashews.** Place the cashews in a bowl just big enough to fit them. Fill with just enough water to cover the almonds. Cover the container and soak the cashews overnight. Drain the cashews the following day and discard the liquid.

2. **Grind.** Place the cashews in a high-quality blender or food processor and process until very finely ground, stopping the blender or food processor and scraping down the sides occasionally. Add the remaining ingredients, and pulse a few times to incorporate.

3. **Strain.** Line a deep bowl, pot, or pitcher with one layer of cheesecloth. Pour the Cashew Cream Cheese into the cheesecloth. Gather up the sides so that you are holding onto the cloth like a sack. Tie the top of the sack to the center of a wooden spoon, and place the spoon across the deep bowl, so that the cheesecloth hangs over the bowl without touching the bottom. This technique drains the liquid and yields a firmer cheese. Drain for 12–24 hours at room temperature. The longer it drains, the firmer it will be. Keep Cashew Cream Cheese in an airtight container in the refrigerator for up to 1 week.

Tofu Ricotta

Dairy-free cheese doesn't get much simpler than this tasty tofu-based concoction. Use in dairy-free lasagna, homemade ravioli, or any dish that calls for ricotta.

YIELD: 1½–2 CUPS (375–500 G)

1 pound (454 g) extra-firm tofu,
    drained and pressed
1½ tablespoons (20 mL) extra-virgin olive oil
2 tablespoons (30 g) nutritional yeast
1 teaspoon lemon juice
½ teaspoon sea salt

1. **Make the cheese.** Place the tofu into a small bowl and crumble it with your fingers. Add the remaining ingredients, stirring everything together until well mixed. Place in the refrigerator for 1–2 hours.

2. **Strain.** Line a small bowl with one layer of cheesecloth. Pour the ricotta into the bowl. Gather up the sides of the cheesecloth and press out some but not all of the liquid. Discard the liquid. Keep Tofu Ricotta in an airtight container in the refrigerator for up to 5 days.

Almond Yogurt

This easy yogurt recipe comes together overnight and tastes better than anything you'll find in a store. Experiment with sweeteners and other flavorings such as vanilla, as well as resting times; the longer your Almond Yogurt sits, the more tart it becomes.

YIELD: 5½ CUPS (1.2 KG)

5 cups (1.2 L) plain, unsweetened almond milk, store-bought or homemade (page 49)

2 tablespoons (30 g) unsweetened cane sugar

¼ teaspoon pectin

6 tablespoons (90 mL) prepared almond yogurt or other dairy-free yogurt

(1) **Prepare.** Make sure your yogurt maker and all your jars and utensils are clean, sterilized, and dry.

(2) **Make the base.** Combine the almond milk and sugar in a medium-large saucepan over medium-high heat. Heat, stirring often, until a candy thermometer inserted into the liquid reads 180°F (82°C). Transfer the liquid to a blender. Add the pectin and blend immediately for 3–4 minutes until slightly thickened (this is important or your pectin will clump together). Transfer to a heat-proof bowl. Clip the thermometer to the bowl and cool the milk to 100°–105°F (around 38°C). (If your milk is too warm, you will kill the active ingredients in the "starter" yogurt.)

(3) **Mix well.** Add the prepared almond yogurt. Mix well, then transfer the yogurt to the sterilized jars, leaving about 1 inch (2.5 cm) of room at the top. Leave the lids off, and use the yogurt maker according to the manufacturer's instructions. (My almond yogurt sits for about 11 hours, but your yogurt maker's instructions may be different.)

(4) **Chill.** Place the lids on your yogurt jars and chill. Almond Yogurt will keep for 3–4 days in the refrigerator.

Soy Yogurt

Like Almond Yogurt (page 64), this recipe requires a yogurt maker, but it comes together easily without any thickening agents. Feel free to add fruit, honey, or nuts to your finished yogurt. Experiment with different resting times; the longer your yogurt rests in the yogurt maker, the more tart and thicker it becomes.

YIELD: 5½ CUPS (1.2 KG)

5 cups (1.2 L) plain, unsweetened soymilk, store-bought or homemade (page 54)

2 tablespoons (30 g) unsweetened cane sugar

6 ounces (0.2 kg) prepared soy yogurt or other dairy-free yogurt

1. **Prepare.** Make sure your yogurt maker and all your jars and utensils are clean, sterilized, and dry.

2. **Make the base.** Combine the soymilk and sugar in a medium-large saucepan over medium-high heat. Heat, stirring often, until a candy thermometer inserted into the liquid reads 180°F (82°C). Transfer the liquid to a heat-proof bowl. Clip the thermometer to the bowl and cool the milk to 100°–105°F (around 82°C). (If your milk is too warm, you will kill the live ingredients of the "starter" yogurt.)

3. **Mix well.** Add the prepared soy yogurt. Mix well, then transfer the yogurt to the sterilized jars, leaving about 1 inch (2.5 cm) of room at the top of the jars. Leave the lids off, and use the yogurt maker according to the manufacturer's instructions. (My Soy Yogurt sits for 8–10 hours, but your yogurt maker's instructions may be different.)

4. **Chill.** Place the lids on your yogurt jars and chill. Soy Yogurt will keep for 3–4 days in the refrigerator.

Coconut Yogurt

This delicious dairy-free yogurt doesn't even require a yogurt maker. Coconut milk makes a thick, rich, flavorful yogurt that tastes indulgently healthy. Before making any kind of homemade yogurt, take care to sterilize your equipment properly. Boil your jars, lids, and bands in about 2 inches (5 cm) of water for 5–10 minutes and allow them to cool before using.

YIELD: ABOUT 5 CUPS (1.2 KG)

Three 15-ounce (990 mL) cans full-fat coconut milk, or 4½ cups (1 L) homemade coconut milk

4 tablespoons (60 g) unsweetened cane sugar

1 tablespoon (15 g) pectin

⅓ cup (80 mL) prepared coconut milk yogurt or other dairy-free yogurt

① **Prepare the slow cooker.** Turn a large slow cooker to "warm." Place several kitchen towels around the pot to warm them. Place several sterilized jars (or one large one if it will fit) on a clean surface. Set aside.

③ **Make the base.** Combine the coconut milk and sugar in a medium-large saucepan over medium-high heat. Heat, stirring often, until a candy thermometer inserted into the liquid reads 180°F (82°C). Transfer the liquid to a blender. Add the pectin and blend immediately for 3–4 minutes until slightly thickened (this is important, or your pectin will clump together). Transfer to a heat-proof bowl. Clip the thermometer to the bowl and cool the mixture to 100°–105°F (around 38°C). (If your mixture is too warm, you will kill the active ingredients in the "starter" yogurt.)

③ **Mix well.** Add the prepared yogurt. Mix well, then transfer the yogurt to the sterilized jars, leaving about 1 inch (2.5 cm) of room at the top. Leave the lids off.

④ **Turn off the slow cooker.** Wrap the jars loosely in the warm kitchen towels and place them upright in the slow cooker. Cover, seal, and let the yogurt rest undisturbed for 12–15 hours (I make this early in the evening and let it sit overnight). Place the lids on your yogurt jars and chill. Coconut Yogurt will keep for 3–4 days in the refrigerator.

Margarine

Making your own margarine is actually very easy—it just requires a little bit of melting and stirring time. Experiment by adding herbs and spices to your margarine for variety. A teaspoon of curry powder adds a lovely, fragrant flavor, and a tablespoon of dried herbs or ¼ cup (10 g) or so of fresh herbs can liven up your homemade spread.

YIELD: ABOUT 2½ CUPS (467 G)

1 cup (236 mL) plus 2 tablespoons (30 mL) room-temperature coconut oil

¾ cup (180 mL) canola oil

½ cup (120 mL) full-fat coconut milk

2-3 teaspoons (4-7 g) ground turmeric

1 teaspoon Dijon mustard

½ teaspoon salt

(1) **Prepare.** Fill the bottom of a double boiler or a small saucepan with several inches (centimeters) of hot water and bring to a simmer. Fill a bowl with ice water and set aside.

(2) **Make the margarine.** Combine the coconut oil and canola oil in the top of a double boiler or a heat-proof bowl. (If using a heat-proof bowl and saucepan, set the bowl over the simmering water but do not let the bottom of the bowl touch the water or the sides of the saucepan.) Let the coconut oil melt completely. Add the remaining ingredients. Stir constantly to combine. Cook, continuing to stir constantly, until a candy thermometer clipped to the side of the bowl reads 120°F (49°C).

(3) **Cool.** Place the bowl into the ice water bath. Stir constantly until the margarine thickens slightly. Transfer the margarine to an airtight container, cover, and refrigerate. Homemade Margarine will keep for up to 2 weeks. (I like to use a mini loaf pan lined with plastic wrap as my container to give my margarine that rectangular shape.)

Chapter 9

BREAKFAST AND BRUNCH

BREAKFAST IS THE MEAL that sets a day of eating—healthy or otherwise—in motion, and brunch is one of life's greatest luxuries. Many traditional recipes for both everyday mornings and special occasions contain milk, butter, cream, and other dairy ingredients, but they don't have to.

Substituting milk with a plant-based milk; swapping butter for coconut oil, heart-healthy oils, or nonhydrogenated margarine; and replacing cheese with homemade Cashew Cheese (page 58) makes the recipes in this chapter healthier, yet just as tasty. You'll find flaky quiche crusts, fluffy pancakes, and banana bread that melt in your mouth—all of it dairy free. Of course, there are recipes for decadent days, too, such as Cream-Filled Yeast Doughnuts (page 82).

Best-Ever Banana Bread

This banana bread bursts with banana flavor and accents of maple and coconut. Not only is it delicious, dairy free or otherwise, but it is also made with healthier ingredients than traditional butter-based breads.

YIELD: ONE 9 X 5-INCH (23 X 13 CM) LOAF, 8-10 SLICES

½ cup (120 mL) plain coconut milk or almond milk, at room temperature

1 teaspoon apple cider vinegar or white wine vinegar

2 cups (250 g) all-purpose flour

¾ cup (150 g) granulated sugar (preferably unrefined cane sugar)

¾ teaspoon baking soda

¾ teaspoon ground cinnamon

¾ teaspoon salt

2 cups (450 g) mashed bananas, from 4–5 large very ripe bananas

½ cup (120 mL) plus 2 tablespoons (30 mL) maple syrup, at room temperature

¼ cup (60 mL) extra-virgin coconut oil, melted

1 teaspoon vanilla extract

① **Prepare.** Preheat the oven to 350°F (180°C, or gas mark 4). Lightly oil a 9 x 5-inch (23 x 13 cm) loaf pan. In a small bowl or cup, combine the coconut milk and cider vinegar.

② **Combine the dry ingredients, then the wet ingredients.** In a medium bowl, mix together the flour, sugar, baking soda, ground cinnamon, and salt. Add the coconut milk mixture, mashed bananas, maple syrup, coconut oil, and vanilla extract, and mix until just combined. Pour the batter into the prepared loaf pan.

③ **Bake.** Bake on the center oven rack for 1 hour, or until a toothpick inserted into the center comes out clean. Cool in the pan for 20 minutes before transferring to a wire cooling rack to cool completely. Serve warm or at room temperature.

Blueberry Cornmeal Muffins

These light, bright muffins are dairy free, gluten free, and soy free, which makes them wonderful for serving larger groups with varied diets. You can make 12 standard-size muffins, or use a mini muffin tin to yield 24 mini muffins—just reduce your baking time to 12 minutes. Xanthan gum is available at health food stores, specialty stores, and online.

YIELD: 12 MUFFINS (24 MINI MUFFINS)

1¾ cups (200 g) all-purpose gluten-free flour

½ cup (70 g) gluten-free cornmeal

2 teaspoons aluminum-free baking powder

1 teaspoon xanthan gum

½ teaspoon baking soda

1 teaspoon salt

1 teaspoon ground cinnamon

⅔ cup (156 mL) canola oil or olive oil

⅓ cup (75 g) packed light brown sugar

3 large organic eggs

½ cup (120 mL) maple syrup

⅔ cup (160 mL) unsweetened almond milk or coconut milk

1 cup fresh (145 g) or frozen (155 g) blueberries

① **Prepare.** Preheat the oven to 325°F (170°C, or gas mark 3). Line a standard 12-cup muffin tin with paper liners.

② **Make the batter.** In a medium bowl, combine the gluten-free flour, cornmeal, baking powder, xanthan gum, baking soda, salt, and ground cinnamon. Create a well in the center of the dry ingredients and add the oil, light brown sugar, eggs, maple syrup, and almond milk or coconut milk. Mix until well combined. Gently fold in the blueberries with a spatula until they are evenly distributed throughout the batter. Portion the batter into the prepared muffin tin, filling each liner about three-quarters full.

③ **Bake the muffins.** Bake for 20–22 minutes, or until the top of the muffin springs back slightly when touched. Cool muffins in the pan for 15–20 minutes before transferring them to a wire cooling rack to cool completely. Serve warm or at room temperature.

Buttermilk Biscuits with Mushroom Gravy

Flaky, melt-in-your mouth biscuits with luscious, flavorful gravy—without butter? It's true! No one will guess that this easy-to-make brunch dish is dairy-free and vegan. A key to perfect biscuits is making sure all your ingredients are very cold beforehand. I like to quadruple this recipe and keep my dry ingredients in the refrigerator as a quick-solution baking mix.

YIELD: MAKES 8 BISCUITS, 4 SERVINGS

FOR THE BISCUITS:

3 cups (411 g) all-purpose flour, plus more if needed

4 teaspoons (10 g) baking powder

½ teaspoon baking soda

1½ teaspoons sea salt

¾ cup (170 g) nonhydrogenated dairy-free soy margarine

1½ cups (255 mL) unsweetened almond or soymilk, cold

1½ tablespoons (22 mL) apple cider vinegar

FOR THE MUSHROOM GRAVY:

1 tablespoon (15 mL) plus ¼ cup (60 mL) extra-virgin coconut oil, divided

1 medium yellow onion, finely chopped

2 cloves garlic, finely minced

1 teaspoon dried thyme

2 cups (132 g) chopped cremini mushrooms

¼ cup (30 g) all-purpose flour

2 cups (0.5 L) unsweetened almond milk or soymilk

½ cup (120 mL) low-sodium vegetable broth

¼ teaspoon sea salt, plus more to taste

Freshly ground black pepper

① **Combine the biscuit ingredients.** In a large bowl, combine the flour, baking powder, baking soda, and sea salt. Using a pastry cutter, two butter knives, or your fingers, cut in the dairy-free soy margarine until the mixture comes together into pea-size granules. Cover and chill for 30 minutes. In a small bowl or cup, whisk together the almond milk (or soymilk) with the cider vinegar, and chill.

② **Prepare.** Preheat the oven to 375°F (190°C, or gas mark 5). Line a large baking sheet with parchment paper.

③ **Make the biscuits.** Lightly flour a clean work surface and metal bench scraper (or offset spatula or knife). Add the almond milk mixture gradually to the dry ingredients until the dough is sticky but does not stick to your hands. Turn out the dough onto the floured work surface and, working quickly, shape the dough into a large rectangle 2 inches (5 cm) thick. Flatten the top slightly with your hands, but avoid overworking the dough—less is more when it comes to biscuits. Using the floured bench scraper or knife, trim the edges of the dough in quick, even, singular motions to create a flat edge all the way around. With quick, even, singular cuts, cut the rectangle into 8 squares, flouring the bench scraper as needed.

Using the floured bench scraper, lift and place each square onto the prepared baking sheet at least 2 inches (5 cm) apart from one another. Bake for 20–25 minutes, or until the biscuits are golden brown.

④ **Make the gravy.** In a large heavy-bottomed skillet over medium-high heat, heat 1 tablespoon (15 mL) of the coconut oil. Add the onion, garlic, and thyme, and cook, stirring frequently, until the onions are soft and fragrant. Add the chopped mushrooms and remaining ¼ cup (60 mL) coconut oil, and cook for 1–2 minutes more. Stirring constantly and vigorously, add the flour and cook for 1 minute, taking care not to let the flour brown. (It should smell toasty.) Gradually add the almond milk, stirring constantly, and then add the vegetable broth. Add the salt, turn the heat to low, and cook until the gravy thickens, 3–5 minutes. Add salt and freshly ground black pepper to taste and serve immediately with the biscuits.

Baked Oatmeal with Spiced Apples

This comforting dish is a healthier version of the Amish classic traditionally prepared with butter, eggs, and milk. Feel free to substitute the apples for another fruit of your choice; pears and any kind of berries make lovely stand-ins. Serve with a splash of almond milk.

YIELD: 8 SERVINGS

1 cup (150 g) peeled apple chunks, ½–1 inch (1–2.5 cm) long

2 tablespoons (30 mL) fresh lemon juice

2 tablespoons (30 g) organic cane sugar

2 cups (160 g) one-minute oats

1 cup (80 g) rolled oats (also known as old-fashioned oats)

½ cup (115 g) packed brown sugar

2 teaspoons baking powder

½ teaspoon cinnamon

¼ teaspoon ground ginger

¾ teaspoon salt

3 tablespoons (21 g) flax meal

¼ cup (60 mL) warm water

1 cup (235 mL) unsweetened almond milk, at room temperature, plus more for serving

⅓ cup (80 mL) pure maple syrup, at room temperature

¼ cup (60 mL) warm extra-virgin coconut oil

① **Prepare.** Preheat the oven to 350°F (180°C, or gas mark 4). Lightly oil an 8 x 8-inch (20 x 20 cm) square baking dish. In a small bowl, toss the apple pieces with the fresh lemon juice and cane sugar.

② **Mix the dry ingredients.** In a medium bowl, stir together the one-minute oats, rolled oats, brown sugar, baking powder, cinnamon, ground ginger, and salt.

③ **Mix the wet ingredients.** In a cup or small bowl, whisk together the flax meal and warm water until the mixture has a goopy consistency. In a medium bowl, combine the almond milk, maple syrup, and warm coconut oil.

④ **Assemble and bake.** Combine the flax mixture and the wet ingredients, then add the wet to the dry ingredients, stirring just to combine. Fold in the apples until evenly distributed throughout, then spread the batter into the prepared dish. Bake for 35–40 minutes, or until a toothpick inserted into the center comes out clean. Cool for 10 minutes, then cut into 8 squares and serve with almond milk.

Carrot Glory Muffins

These muffins really are glorious and chock-full of good things. Coconut oil, honey, apples, pecans, and freshly grated carrots make a healthy treat for on-the-go mornings or special brunches.

YIELD: 18 MUFFINS

1 cup (125 g) all-purpose flour

1 cup (125 g) whole-wheat flour

½ cup (40 g) rolled oats

½ cup (100 g) organic cane sugar

2 teaspoons (10 g) baking soda

2 teaspoons (10 g) ground cinnamon

½ teaspoon sea salt

½ cup (60 g) dried cranberries or golden raisins

½ cup (55 g) chopped pecans

½ cup (40 g) shredded unsweetened coconut

2 cups (220 g) grated carrot

3 large eggs, lightly beaten

½ cup (120 mL) warm coconut oil
  or extra virgin olive oil

½ cup (160 mL) honey

2 teaspoons (10 mL) vanilla extract

1 green apple, finely grated

½ cup (123 g) unsweetened applesauce

1. **Prepare.** Preheat the oven to 350°F (180°C, or gas mark 4). Grease 18 cups in 2 standard-size muffin tins with coconut oil.

2. **Make the batter.** In a large bowl, mix together the flours, oats, sugar, baking soda, cinnamon, and sea salt. Fold in the cranberries, pecans, coconut, and grated carrot. In another bowl, whisk together the eggs, warm coconut oil, honey, and vanilla extract. Add the grated apple and applesauce and mix well. Add the wet ingredients to the dry ingredients, and stir until the batter is just combined.

3. **Fill the muffin tins and bake.** Portion the batter into the prepared muffin tins, filling each cup about three-quarters full. Bake for 15–20 minutes, or until a toothpick inserted into the center of a muffin comes out clean. Cool muffins for 5–10 minutes in the tin before transferring them to a wire cooling rack to cool completely.

Broiled Grapefruit with Honey Coconut Yogurt

Broiled grapefruit is a treat, and especially when served with homemade coconut yogurt and honey. Serve this for a special brunch with edible flowers, such as nasturtiums, or make the coconut yogurt ahead of time and broil the grapefruit on busy workday mornings when you're inclined to skip breakfast.

YIELD: 4 SERVINGS

FOR THE BROILED GRAPEFRUITS:

2 large grapefruits, halved
¼ cup (50 g) organic cane sugar or raw sugar
Dash of cinnamon
Pinch of sea salt

FOR THE HONEY COCONUT YOGURT:

2 cups (460 g) Coconut Yogurt (page 66)
3 tablespoons (45 mL) honey, or to taste
Edible flowers for garnish (optional)

1. **Broil the grapefruits.** Preheat the broiler. Slice a sliver off of the bottom of each of the grapefruit halves so they sit flat. Place the grapefruits face up on a baking sheet. In a small bowl or cup, combine the sugar, cinnamon, and salt, and sprinkle evenly on each of the halves. Broil for 7–10 minutes, or until the sugar melts and begins to caramelize. Cool the halves for 5–10 minutes.

2. **Make the topping.** Meanwhile, mix the Coconut Yogurt and honey in a small bowl. Serve each half of broiled grapefruit with a generous dollop of yogurt and edible flowers (if using).

Buckwheat Blueberry Pancakes

Fluffy, cheerful, and healthy, these hotcakes are perfect for summer brunches when blueberries are in season. Coconut oil gives these pancakes a rich, sweet undertone that complements hearty buckwheat and tart blueberries. Letting your batter rest on the counter for 15–20 minutes makes a fluffier, less-grainy pancake by allowing the glutens to relax slightly.

YIELD: 10–12 PANCAKES, 4–6 SERVINGS

½ cup (60 g) all-purpose flour

½ cup (60 g) buckwheat flour

½ cup (62 g) whole-wheat flour

1 tablespoon (15 g) baking powder

¼ teaspoon salt

1 large egg, lightly beaten

1 cup (235 mL) almond milk, at room temperature

3 tablespoons (45 g) warm extra-virgin coconut oil

2 tablespoons (30 mL) pure maple syrup or honey

½ cup (74 g) fresh blueberries (substitute frozen if necessary)

Coconut oil and maple syrup, for serving

① **Mix the dry ingredients, then the wet.** In a medium bowl, sift together the flours. Mix in the baking powder and salt. In another medium bowl, mix together the egg, almond milk, melted coconut oil, and syrup. Add the wet ingredients to the dry, mixing just to combine. Fold in the blueberries. Let rest for 15–20 minutes.

② **Make the pancakes.** Heat a lightly oiled frying pan or griddle over medium heat. Ladle the batter onto the griddle, ¼ cup (60 mL) for each pancake. Once bubbles appear on the surfaces of the pancakes (after about 2 minutes), gently slide a spatula beneath them and flip to cook the other sides. Repeat until all the batter is used. Serve immediately.

Cinnamon Rolls

Few things are as delightfully indulgent as a pan of freshly baked cinnamon rolls. This recipe is quicker than overnight cinnamon roll recipes, so you can prepare your cinnamon rolls and eat them the same morning.

YIELD: 12 ROLLS

FOR THE ROLLS:

¾ cup (175 mL) coconut milk or almond milk

¼ cup (60 mL) extra-virgin coconut oil

One ¼-ounce (7 g) package yeast

¼ cup (50 g) organic cane sugar

3¼ cups (390 g) all-purpose flour, divided

½ teaspoon salt

1 large egg, lightly beaten

¼ cup (60 mL) water, at room temperature

FOR THE CINNAMON FILLING:

1 cup (200 g) packed brown sugar

1 tablespoon (15 g) ground cinnamon

½ cup (120 mL) coconut oil, at room temperature (not liquid)

½ cup (55 g) chopped pecans

½ cup (72 g) raisins

① **Prepare the rolls.** Combine the coconut milk and the coconut oil in a small saucepan over medium heat. Heat until the milk is lukewarm and the coconut oil is completely melted. If the milk is hotter than lukewarm (90°F [32°C]), cool it for a few minutes (if it is too hot, it will kill the yeast). In a large bowl or the bowl of a stand mixer, combine the yeast, sugar, and lukewarm dairy-free milk. Let stand for 5 minutes or until slightly bubbly. Add 2 cups (240 g) of the flour, salt, egg, and water. Mix well to combine. Gradually add the remaining 1¼ cups (150 g) flour, ½ cup (60 g) at a time,

stirring well with each addition. When the dough pulls away from the sides of the bowl, turn it out onto a lightly floured surface and knead until elastic and smooth, about 5 minutes. Cover the dough with a warm, damp kitchen towel and let it rest for 30 minutes.

② **Roll out the rolls and make the filling.** Lightly grease a standard 12-cup muffin tin. Punch down the dough and transfer to a lightly floured surface. Roll out the dough into a large 12 x 10-inch (30.5 x 25 cm) rectangle. In a small cup, combine the brown sugar, cinnamon, and coconut oil. Spread the cinnamon filling onto the dough, and sprinkle with the chopped pecans and raisins. Starting with one of the long sides, roll up the dough like a piece of paper and pinch to seal. Using a sharp knife or bench scraper, cut the roll into 12 equal pieces. Place the rolls cut-side-up in the muffin tins. Cover and let rise again until doubled in size, about 30 minutes.

③ **Bake.** Preheat the oven to 375°F (190°C, or gas mark 5). Bake the rolls for 20–25 minutes, or until golden brown. Serve warm.

Cream-Filled Yeast Doughnuts

Doughnuts are one of those things that taste so much better fried, which, for a general health nut, can be hard to admit. Filled with a coconut milk pastry cream, these doughnuts will remind you that even on a healthy diet, sometimes you just want something decadent. Feel free to substitute jelly for the Coconut Milk Pastry Cream for jelly doughnut lovers.

YIELD: 12-16 DOUGHNUTS

FOR THE COCONUT MILK PASTRY CREAM:

⅔ cup (150 g) organic cane sugar

⅓ cup (40 g) flour

½ teaspoon sea salt

6 large organic egg yolks

2 cups (475 mL) full-fat coconut milk

1 teaspoon vanilla extract

FOR THE YEAST DOUGHNUTS:

2 tablespoons (24 g) active dry yeast

½ cup (120 mL) unsweetened almond milk
  (or soymilk or hemp milk), warmed

2½ cups (310 g) all-purpose flour, plus more
  as needed

5 tablespoons (65 g) organic cane sugar,
  plus more for coating

2 teaspoons (12 g) sea salt

2 large eggs

3 tablespoons (45 g) melted extra-virgin coconut oil

Canola oil, for frying

① **Make the pastry cream.** Set a fine-mesh strainer over a small heat-proof bowl. In a small bowl, mix together the sugar, flour, and sea salt. In a medium bowl, whisk the egg yolks well. Gradually add the sugar mixture to the egg, beating until the mixture is thick.

Place the coconut milk in a medium saucepan over medium-high heat. Heat the milk until steam just begins to rise from the surface but the coconut milk is not boiling, about 3-4 minutes. Remove from the heat and add the vanilla, then slowly whisk the coconut milk into the egg mixture, whisking constantly to avoid cooking the eggs.

Pour the cream into the saucepan and heat over medium heat. Continue whisking constantly for 3-4 minutes and bring the cream to a low boil. Remove immediately from the heat and pour through the fine-mesh strainer into the small heat-proof bowl. Press plastic wrap directly onto the surface of the cream to prevent skin from forming. Refrigerate for 4 hours or overnight.

② **Make the dough.** In the bowl of a stand mixer with a dough hook attachment or a large bowl, combine the yeast and warm almond milk and let stand until bubbles form on the surface, 2-5 minutes. Add the flour, sugar, salt, and eggs and mix until the dough starts to come together and pull away from the sides of the bowl, starting at a low speed and working up to medium (if doing this by hand, just work the dough until it comes together). Add the coconut oil 1 tablespoon (15 mL) at a time, mixing well with each addition, until fully incorporated. Turn the dough out onto a lightly floured surface and knead until the dough is soft and elastic, adding flour as needed until the dough does not stick to your hands but is not dry. Return the dough to the bowl, cover, and set in a warm place until doubled in size, about 1½ hours.

③ **Make the doughnuts.** Lightly flour a large baking sheet, a bench scraper or spatula, and a round biscuit cutter or a glass. Turn out the dough onto a lightly floured work surface and form into a rectangle about ½ inch (1.3 cm) thick. Use a floured biscuit cutter to cut 12–16 doughnuts and transfer these to the prepared baking sheet using the bench scraper. Cover the doughnuts with plastic wrap and let them rise for another 15–30 minutes.

④ **Fry the doughnuts.** Line a large baking sheet with paper towels. Fill a large, heavy-bottomed saucepan with about 3 inches (7.5 cm) of canola oil and heat over medium-high heat. When the oil reaches 370°F (188°C) on a deep fry or candy thermometer, gently place the doughnuts in the oil, taking care not to let them touch one another. Fry the doughnuts for about 1 minute, or until golden brown on both sides. Use a slotted spoon to remove the doughnuts from the oil. Place on the paper towel–lined baking sheet. Pour a small amount (½–1 cup [100–200 g]) of sugar into a bowl. Cool the doughnuts until just cool enough to touch but still warm, and then gently toss them in sugar. Let the doughnuts cool completely, about 45 minutes.

⑤ **Fill the doughnuts.** Transfer the Coconut Milk Pastry Cream to a pastry bag with a small round tip. Using the tip of a sharp knife or a toothpick, poke a hole in the side of each of the doughnuts. Insert the tip of the pastry bag into the hole and fill each doughnut with several tablespoons of Coconut Milk Pastry Cream. Serve immediately.

Dairy-Free Quiche Lorraine

Conventionally farmed eggs simply cannot compete with organic eggs when it comes to taste, so even if you don't ordinarily purchase organic products, you might want to for this dish. When preparing the crust, keep all of your ingredients very cold to achieve the flakiest crust possible.

YIELD: ONE 9-INCH (23 CM) QUICHE, 8 SERVINGS

FOR THE CRUST:

1¼ cups (155 g) all-purpose flour

1 teaspoon organic cane sugar

½ teaspoon salt

½ cup (113 g) nonhydrogenated soy margarine, cut into pieces and very cold

2-4 tablespoons (30 mL) very cold water

FOR THE FILLING:

8 ounces (227 g) organic nitrate-free turkey bacon

6 large eggs, preferably organic

1½ cups (355 mL) plain unsweetened soymilk

½ teaspoon freshly ground black pepper

¼ teaspoon salt

1 cup (120 g) grated Cashew Cheese (page 58) or other grated dairy-free cheese, divided

① **Prepare the crust.** In a medium bowl, sift together the flour, sugar, and salt. Cut in the soy margarine using a pastry cutter or your fingers until your mixture resembles a crumbly fine meal. Add the cold water, 1 tablespoon (15 mL) at a time, until your dough just comes together and is not too sticky or too dry (if it is just a little sticky at this point, it's okay). Turn the dough out onto a lightly floured surface, and knead for a minute or so until the dough feels satiny. Wrap tightly in plastic wrap and chill for 1-2 hours. (If you freeze or refrigerate the dough for longer, let the dough soften slightly before rolling it out.)

② **Bake.** Preheat the oven to 375°F (190°C, or gas mark 5). Lightly grease a 9-inch (23 cm) pie plate with soy margarine. Turn out the dough onto a lightly floured surface. Using a rolling pin, roll out the dough to about ⅛ inch (3 mm) thick, and carefully transfer to the prepared pie plate. Fit the dough into the pie plate and pinch a crust around the edge with your fingers. Prick the bottom of the dough in several places with a fork and place the crust into the freezer while preparing the quiche filling.

③ **Make the filling.** In a heavy-bottomed skillet over medium heat, cook the bacon for 5-7 minutes or until crisp, flipping as needed. Transfer to a paper towel–lined plate to cool slightly, then chop coarsely. Meanwhile, whisk the eggs in a medium bowl. Add the soymilk, pepper, and salt, whisking well to combine. Whisk in half of the Cashew Cheese. Remove the pie plate from the freezer. Arrange the bacon pieces on top of the crust, then sprinkle the remaining half of the Cashew Cheese on top of the bacon. Pour the filling slowly over the bacon and Cashew Cheese. Place the pie on the center rack in the oven and bake for 35-40 minutes, or until the center is no longer jiggly. Cool the quiche for 15 minutes before serving. Serve hot.

Homemade Almond Yogurt with Cinnamon Granola and Fruit

Nothing will make your home smell better than the aroma of this granola as it bakes. This recipe makes a lot, so keep it stored in an airtight container at room temperature for up to 2 months. Serve ½ cup (120 g) of granola sprinkled over fruit and homemade Almond Yogurt for a quick, healthy breakfast during the week.

YIELD: 14–15 CUPS (3.5–3.75 KG), ABOUT 25 SERVINGS

FOR THE CINNAMON GRANOLA:

8 cups (640 g) rolled oats

1 cup (100 g) millet

½ cup (28 g) wheat germ

1 cup (110 g) finely chopped almonds

1 cup (110 g) finely chopped pecans

1 cup (140 g) raw sunflower seeds

½ cup (115 g) packed organic brown sugar

1 tablespoon (2.3 g) ground cinnamon

1½ teaspoons salt

½ cup (120 mL) warm coconut oil

½ cup (120 mL) canola oil

1 cup (226 mL) maple syrup

1 teaspoon vanilla extract

2 cups (240 mL) dried cranberries or other dried fruit

FOR THE FRUIT AND YOGURT:

Sliced bananas

Fresh strawberries, hulled and halved

Almond Yogurt (page 64), to serve

Honey or maple syrup, to taste (optional)

1. **Prepare the granola.** Preheat the oven to 325°F (170°C, or gas mark 3). Lightly oil 2 large baking sheets. In a large bowl, mix together the oats, millet, wheat germ, almonds, pecans, sunflower seeds, organic brown sugar, cinnamon, and salt until well combined. In another bowl, whisk together the warm coconut oil, canola oil, maple syrup, and vanilla extract. Add the liquid ingredients to the oats and nuts, and mix well until coated evenly. Spread the mixture evenly onto the 2 prepared pans and bake for 20–30 minutes, rotating the pans halfway through. Cool completely on the pans, then transfer to a large bowl, and stir in the dried cranberries. Store at room temperature in an airtight container.

2. **Serve.** Serve granola with sliced banana, fresh strawberries, Almond Yogurt, and a drizzle of honey or maple syrup.

French Toast Casserole

Challah, a traditional Jewish egg bread, is almost always dairy free. Thick and rich, it's perfect for dishes like this French toast casserole. Because this casserole rests overnight, it is a breeze for weekend brunches—just prepare it the night before, and then top it with the crumble and pop it in the oven the following morning.

YIELD: 6–8 SERVINGS

FOR THE CASSEROLE:

1 large loaf challah (about 14–16 ounces [397–454 g]), sliced into 1-inch (2.5 cm)-thick slices

9 large organic eggs

1½ cups (355 mL) full-fat coconut milk

1½ cups (355 mL) plain unsweetened almond milk

2 tablespoons (30 g) organic cane sugar (optional)

1 teaspoon pure vanilla extract

½ teaspoon ground cinnamon

⅛ teaspoon salt

FOR THE MAPLE TOPPING:

½ cup (120 mL) coconut oil, at room temperature

¼ cup (60 g) packed brown sugar

¼ cup (60 mL) pure maple syrup, plus more for serving

½ cup (55 g) finely chopped pecans

(1) **Prepare the casserole.** Grease a 9 x 13-inch (23 x 33 cm) casserole dish with coconut oil. Overlap the bread slices in the dish in one uneven layer. Whisk the eggs slightly in a large bowl. Add the coconut milk, almond milk, sugar, vanilla extract, cinnamon, and salt, and whisk until well combined. Pour the egg mixture evenly over the bread. Cover the dish with plastic wrap and place in the refrigerator overnight.

(2) **Bake the casserole and make the topping.** Preheat the oven to 350°F (180°C, or gas mark 4). In a small bowl, combine the coconut oil, brown sugar, maple syrup, and pecans. Remove the casserole from the refrigerator and spread the topping evenly over the bread slices. Bake until the casserole is puffed up and golden brown, 35–45 minutes. Serve immediately with maple syrup.

Maple Walnut Sugar Scones

Full of fall flavors, these scones are perfect for the autumn holidays. Walnuts and whole-wheat flour pair with maple and coconut to create a layered taste that will impress any dairy-free or vegan skeptic.

YIELD: 8-10 SCONES

1¾ cups (215 g) whole-wheat pastry flour

½ cup (60 g) all-purpose flour

1 cup (80 g) rolled oats

½ cup (55 g) finely chopped walnuts

2 tablespoons (30 g) baking powder

½ teaspoon sea salt

½ cup (113 g) nonhydrogenated soy margarine at room temperature

¼ cup (60 mL) unrefined coconut oil, at room temperature

½ cup (120 mL) coconut milk

⅓ cup (80 mL) pure maple syrup, at room temperature

Coconut cream, for brushing

¼-⅓ cup (60-75 g) unrefined cane sugar, for sprinkling

¼ cup (50 g) brown sugar, for topping

① **Make the dough.** Preheat the oven to 400°F (200°C, or gas mark 6). Line a large baking sheet with parchment paper and set aside. Place the flours, oats, walnuts, baking powder, and sea salt in a food processor, and pulse until well mixed. Add the soy margarine by the tablespoon (14 g) and the coconut oil, pulsing until the mixture resembles a fine, crumbly meal. In a small bowl, whisk together the coconut milk and maple syrup, and then add this liquid to the flour mixture gradually. Pulse until the dough just comes together.

② **Cut out the scones.** Turn the dough out onto a lightly floured work surface, and roll into a rectangle about 1 inch (2.5 cm) thick. Using a floured bench scraper or sharp knife, trim the edges of the dough in quick, even, singular motions to create a flat edge all the way around. With quick, even, singular cuts, cut the rectangle into 8-10 triangles or squares, flouring the bench scraper as needed. Transfer these to the prepared baking sheet using a spatula or bench scraper, and place 2 inches (5 cm) apart from one another. Brush the scones lightly with coconut cream, then sprinkle each generously with the unrefined cane sugar.

③ **Bake.** Bake for 20 minutes, or until the scones are golden brown. Sprinkle with the brown sugar immediately, then cool the scones slightly before serving. Serve warm or at room temperature.

Vegetable Quiche with Buckwheat Crust

This dairy-free, gluten-free, and soy-free quiche is perfect for people with multiple allergies but still delicious for everyone else, and the no-roll crust is a great solution for busy cooks. Experiment with other fresh seasonal herbs and vegetables to make it your own.

YIELD: ONE 9-INCH (23 CM) QUICHE, 8 SERVINGS

FOR THE CRUST:

1½ cups (185 g) buckwheat flour

½ teaspoon salt

½ cup (120 mL) virgin coconut oil, room temperature

2–3 tablespoons (30–45 mL) room-temperature water

FOR THE VEGETABLE FILLING:

2 tablespoons (30 mL) coconut oil

1 medium yellow onion, finely chopped

2 cloves garlic, finely minced

1 red bell pepper, cored and chopped or sliced

1 cup (70 g) sliced cremini mushrooms

¼ cup (10 g) finely chopped fresh basil

6 large organic eggs

1½ cups (355 mL) soymilk

½ teaspoon sea salt

1 cup (30 g) fresh baby spinach, stems removed

① **Prepare the crust.** In a food processor, combine the buckwheat flour and salt, pulsing just a few times to mix. Add the coconut oil, pulsing just to combine. Add the water, 1 tablespoon (15 mL) at a time, until the dough just comes together.

② **Form the crust.** Preheat the oven to 375°F (190°C, or gas mark 5). Lightly oil a 9-inch (23 cm) pie plate. Press the dough into the prepared pie plate, smoothing it with your fingers as much as you can. Place the dish in the freezer while preparing the filling.

③ **Make the filling.** Heat the coconut oil in a heavy-bottomed skillet over medium heat. Add the chopped onion and garlic and cook, stirring often, until the onions are soft and translucent, 3–5 minutes. Add the bell pepper, and cook for 1–2 minutes, then add the mushrooms. Cook for 2–3 minutes more, stirring often. Remove the pan from the heat, and stir in the fresh basil. Set aside. In a large bowl, whisk the eggs. Whisk in the soymilk and sea salt until well combined. Add the spinach to the other vegetables in the saucepan, then transfer all of the vegetables to the prepared pie crust, spreading them evenly in the dish. Pour the egg mixture over the vegetables.

④ **Bake.** Bake for 35–45 minutes, or until the quiche is lightly browned and not jiggly in the center. Cool the quiche for 15 minutes before serving. Serve hot.

Buttery Vegan Pancakes, Three Ways

Coconut oil makes these vegan pancakes feel luxuriously buttery even though they're dairy free. Enjoy them plain or in Strawberry, Pumpkin, or Cinnamon Banana varieties.

YIELD: 10–12 PANCAKES, 4 SERVINGS

FOR THE PANCAKE BATTER:

1⅔ cups (205 g) all-purpose flour

2 tablespoons (30 g) plus 2 teaspoons (10 g) organic cane sugar

2¾ teaspoons (13 g) baking powder

¾ teaspoon sea salt

1⅔ cups (395 mL) almond milk

2 tablespoons (30 mL) coconut oil, warmed just until melted

½ teaspoon vanilla extract

FOR THE STRAWBERRY VARIATION:

1 cup (170 g) chopped fresh, hulled strawberries

FOR THE PUMPKIN VARIATION:

⅓ cup (82 g) pumpkin puree

1 teaspoon ground cinnamon

½ teaspoon ground ginger

FOR THE CINNAMON BANANA VARIATION:

1 teaspoon ground cinnamon

2 fresh bananas, sliced

Maple syrup or powdered sugar, for serving

① **Prepare the batter.** In a medium-large bowl, combine the flour, sugar, baking powder, and sea salt. In a small bowl, whisk together the almond milk, coconut oil, and vanilla extract. (For Pumpkin Pancakes, also add the pumpkin puree, ground cinnamon, and ground ginger.) Add the wet ingredients to the dry, mixing just until the batter comes together. Do not overmix. Let the batter rest for 10 minutes on the counter to allow the glutens to relax. (For Strawberry Pancakes, fold in fresh strawberries using a spatula or wooden spoon. For Cinnamon Banana Pancakes, stir in cinnamon and then fold in bananas.)

② **Make the pancakes.** Heat a lightly oiled griddle over medium-high heat. Ladle the batter into the pan, about ¼ cup (60 mL) per pancake, and cook until bubbles form on the surface and the edges are firm and dry, about 1–2 minutes. Flip the pancakes and cook until both sides are brown. Repeat until all the batter has been used. Serve immediately with maple syrup or powdered sugar.

Chapter 10

STARTERS AND SOUPS

NEXT TO DESSERTS, appetizers are one of the most trying for people and cooks who are dairy free. Classic starters and snacks often involve cheese, and those quick-and-easy-to-whip-up party dips usually call for cream cheese, sour cream, or milk.

Hors d'oeuvres, starters, first courses, and appetizers are supposed to be celebratory and rich, but they don't have to be loaded with unhealthy fats and artificial ingredients. Instead, the recipes you'll find in this chapter use nuts, coconut, and soy to create healthier savory treats for every occasion.

Cashew Cheese Dip

This creamy, savory dip is delicious served with tortilla chips or veggies as an appetizer or party snack. If you find that grinding nuts is a hardship for your blender, soak the cashews the night before to make blending easier.

YIELD: 3 CUPS (690 G), 8-10 SERVINGS

2½ cups (590 mL) unsweetened almond milk, divided

1 tablespoon (8 g) cornstarch

¼ cup (60 mL) lemon juice

¼ cup (30 g) nutritional yeast

½ teaspoon garlic powder

¼ teaspoon turmeric

2 tablespoons (30 g) tahini

1½ cups (138 g) finely ground cashews

½ cup (125 g) prepared spicy salsa, drained of excess juices

¼ teaspoon sea salt, plus more to taste

(1) **Combine.** Pour 1 cup (235 mL) of the almond milk into a small bowl or cup. Add the cornstarch and stir.

(2) **Cook.** Place the remaining 1½ cups (355 mL) almond milk, lemon juice, nutritional yeast, garlic powder, turmeric, and tahini in a small saucepan over medium heat. Stir to combine, then add the ground cashews and almond–cornstarch mixture. Cook for 1-2 minutes, stirring often, then add the salsa and sea salt. Continue cooking, stirring often, until the dip starts to thicken (the dip will thicken as it cools). Remove the pan from the heat and transfer the dip to a heat-proof bowl. (If preparing ahead of time, press a piece of plastic wrap directly on the surface of the dip before chilling to prevent a skin from forming as it cools.)

Cashew Cheese–Stuffed Jalapeño Poppers

These spicy treats are baked instead of fried and filled with healthy fats from Cashew Cheese and avocado, so you can feel good about serving them to your friends and family. Panko breadcrumbs are almost always dairy free, unlike many commercial breadcrumb products on the market. If these are not available, you can make your own breadcrumbs by simply placing a few slices of day-old bread into a food processor or blender and pulsing until crumbs form.

YIELD: 24 POPPERS, 6-10 SERVINGS

FOR THE PEPPERS AND FILLING:

12 large jalapeño peppers

1 large, ripe avocado, halved

¼ cup (4 g) finely chopped fresh cilantro

1 tablespoon (15 mL) fresh lemon juice

¼–½ teaspoon cayenne pepper, or to taste

½ teaspoon sea salt

2 cups (520 g) grated Cashew Cheese (page 58)

FOR THE BREADING:

½ cup (65 g) flour

2 large eggs

3 tablespoons (45 mL) almond milk or coconut milk

1½ cups (75 g) panko breadcrumbs

2 tablespoons (14 g) paprika

1 tablespoon (15 g) sea salt

1 tablespoon (15 g) cayenne pepper (or to taste)

1 tablespoon (13 g) onion powder

1 tablespoon (8 g) nutritional yeast

① **Prepare.** Preheat the oven to 450°F (230°C, or gas mark 8). Lightly oil a large baking sheet.

② **Stuff the peppers.** Using a sharp paring knife, halve the peppers lengthwise. Remove the seeds, stems, and membranes. (If your hands are at all cracked or dry, use gloves for this part to prevent burning.) Scoop the flesh of the avocado into a small bowl. Mash well with the cilantro, lemon juice, cayenne pepper, and sea salt. Mix in the grated Cashew Cheese until well incorporated. Spoon this filling into the jalapeño halves.

③ **Prepare the breading.** Place the flour in a small bowl. In another small bowl, whisk together the eggs and almond milk until well combined. Place the panko breadcrumbs, paprika, sea salt, cayenne pepper, onion powder, and nutritional yeast in a third small bowl, and stir just to mix.

④ **Make the poppers.** Working with 1 pepper at a time, dredge the peppers in the flour, turning to coat. Next, dip peppers into the egg mixture, turning to coat, and use your thumbs to keep the filling in the peppers as you turn them. Dredge the peppers in the spiced panko, turning and pressing to coat. As you work, place the peppers filling side up onto the prepared baking sheet. Bake until the poppers are golden brown, about 15-20 minutes. Serve immediately.

Creamy Spinach Dip

This dip gets its creamy consistency from coconut, almond milk, and baked potato. I like to make it when I have a leftover baked potato, or if I make a baked potato dish like the Twice-Baked Cheesy Potatoes (page 145) I throw an extra one in the oven.

YIELD: 4 CUPS (920 G), 8–12 APPETIZER-SIZE SERVINGS

1 tablespoon (15 mL) olive oil

1 large yellow onion, finely chopped

3 cloves garlic, minced

One 14-ounce (397 g) can artichoke hearts, drained and coarsely chopped

2 cups (60 g) baby spinach, stems removed and coarsely chopped

¾ cup (175 mL) almond milk, soymilk, or hemp milk

1 cup (230 g) Coconut Sour Cream (page 57)

1 medium baked potato, skinned

1 cup (260 g) grated Cashew Cheese (page 58), divided

Sea salt and freshly ground pepper

① **Prepare.** Preheat the oven to 425°F (220°C, or gas mark 7). Lightly oil an 8 x 8-inch (20 x 20 cm) casserole dish.

② **Cook the vegetables.** In a large saucepan or Dutch oven, heat the olive oil over medium heat. Add the chopped onion and garlic cloves and cook, stirring often, for 3–5 minutes, or until the onions are soft. Add the artichoke hearts and cook for 1 minute, continuing to stir often. Add the spinach a handful at a time, letting one bunch wilt before adding the next, until all of the spinach is wilted, about 4 minutes. Transfer the vegetables to a colander and drain, pressing out any excess liquid. Return the vegetables to the pot. Add the almond milk and Coconut Sour Cream, and stir to combine.

③ **Blend, then bake.** Transfer half of the vegetable mixture and the baked potato to a blender. Blend until creamy and smooth. Return the blended mixture to the saucepan. Fold in ½ cup (130 g) of the Cashew Cheese. Add sea salt and freshly ground pepper to taste. Pour the dip into the prepared casserole dish and sprinkle the remaining ½ cup (130 g) Cashew Cheese evenly over the top. Bake for 20–25 minutes, or until the Cashew Cheese is golden brown. Serve hot.

Dairy-Free Nachos Supreme

This appetizer is not meant to be taken too seriously; versatility is a given, and substitutions and additions are welcome. Feel free to adjust it to suit your tastes. Add refried beans, organic ground beef, vegan meat substitute, or even mango to your supreme creation.

YIELD: 6-8 SERVINGS

FOR THE NACHO CHEESE SAUCE:

2 cups (270 g) raw cashews

1 cup (135 g) raw pine nuts

3 tablespoons (45 mL) lemon juice

½ teaspoon garlic powder

½ teaspoon onion powder

2 teaspoons (12 g) sea salt, plus more to taste

½ cup (60 g) nutritional yeast

3½ cups (800 mL) plain unsweetened almond milk, cashew milk, or soy milk

FOR THE GUACAMOLE:

3 large avocados, peeled and pitted

2 tablespoons (30 mL) fresh lime juice

1 teaspoon sea salt

½ cup (80 g) diced red onion

¼ cup (8 g) finely chopped fresh cilantro

1 tomato, chopped

FOR ASSEMBLY:

1 bag (8 ounces [225 g]) tortilla chips (try organic blue chips)

1 cup (250 g) mild salsa

1 small head lettuce, shredded

2 cups (360 g) chopped tomato

2 cups (200 g) sliced black olives

1 cup (460 g) Cashew Sour Cream (page 57) or Coconut Sour Cream (page 57)

Scallions, for garnish

1. **Prepare the Nacho Cheese Sauce.** Place the cashews and pine nuts in a blender and blend until finely ground. Add the lemon juice, garlic powder, onion powder, sea salt, nutritional yeast, and half of the dairy-free milk, and blend until creamy, adding more dairy-free milk if necessary. Pour the cheese sauce into a small saucepan. Add the remaining dairy-free milk and stir to combine. Heat over medium-high heat until the sauce is hot and slightly thickened, about 2-4 minutes. Remove from the heat to cool slightly before serving.

2. **Prepare the guacamole.** Place the avocados, lime juice, sea salt, red onion, and cilantro in a small bowl, and mash until the avocado is creamy. Fold in the chopped tomato.

3. **Assemble and serve.** Arrange one layer (it doesn't have to be perfectly even) of tortilla chips on a large serving platter. Drizzle some of the Nacho Cheese Sauce over the chips. Top with half the salsa, half the guacamole, half the lettuce, half the tomato, and half the black olives. Add another layer of chips, and pour the remaining Nacho Cheese Sauce over the top, followed by the remaining salsa, guacamole, lettuce, tomato, and black olives. Place dollops of Cashew Sour Cream (or Coconut Sour Cream, if using) over all, and garnish with scallions. Serve immediately.

Dairy-Free Cheese Logs, Three Ways

Set these three logs out at a party then watch as everyone eats them and comes back for seconds. Full of cheese flavor, healthy nutrients, and festive color, these logs are really special, and despite the longish ingredient list, they don't take very much time to prepare.

YIELD: THREE 3 X 5-INCH (7.5 X 13 CM) CHEESE LOGS, SERVES 15 TO 20

FOR THE CHEESE BASE:

2 cups (280 g) raw cashews

½ cup (72 g) raw macadamia nuts

½ cup (60 g) nutritional yeast

1 teaspoon salt

3 cups (705 mL) full-fat coconut milk

½ cup (120 mL) unsweetened almond milk

½ cup (40 g) agar flakes (one 1-ounce [28 g] package)

½ cup (120 mL) canola oil or coconut oil

¼ cup (60 g) white miso

2 tablespoons (30 mL) fresh lemon juice

FOR THE SUN-DRIED TOMATO AND HERB LOG:

¼ cup (28 g) chopped sun-dried tomatoes packed in olive oil

½ teaspoon dried oregano

½ teaspoon garlic powder

1 cup (36 g) finely chopped chives, divided

Pinch of salt

½ cup (30 g) finely chopped fresh Italian parsley

FOR THE CRANBERRY PECAN LOG:

1 cup (120 g) chopped dried cranberries

1 cup (95 g) finely chopped pecans

FOR THE PISTACHIO LOG:

1 cup (92 g) chopped shelled unsalted pistachios

① **Grind the nuts.** Place the cashews and macadamia nuts in a blender or large food processor and process until very finely ground. Add the nutritional yeast and salt and pulse a few times to incorporate.

② **Make the cheese base.** Combine the milks, agar flakes, and oil in a medium saucepan over medium-high heat. Stirring constantly, bring the milk to a simmer then turn down the heat to medium. Continue stirring often for about 10 minutes until the milk thickens slightly. The mixture will start off looking separated, with the oil floating to the top and the agar flakes visible, but should become relatively consistent throughout after cooking. Remove from the heat.

Pour the milk–agar mixture into the blender or food processor and mix with the ground nuts until well blended. Add the miso and fresh lemon juice and blend until smooth.

③ **Chill overnight.** Line 3 mini loaf pans with plastic wrap, leaving about 2 inches (5 cm) of overhang. Press the plastic wrap to adhere to the sides as much as possible. Pour the cashew–macadamia cheese into 2 of the loaf pans, and then with the remaining cheese, make the Sun-Dried Tomato and Herb Log. Mix in the sun-dried tomatoes, dried oregano, garlic powder, ¼ cup (8 g) of the chives, and the extra pinch of salt until just combined. Pour this into the remaining lined loaf pan, cover all 3, and chill overnight.

4. **Finish the cheese logs.** Set out 3 small bowls. In one bowl, mix the remaining ¾ cup (24 g) chives with the chopped parsley. In another bowl, combine the dried cranberries and chopped pecans. In the third bowl, place the chopped pistachios. Lift the cheeses out of the loaf pans by the plastic and invert them onto a cutting board. Coat the Sun-Dried Tomato Cheese Log in the chives and parsley, pressing with your hands to evenly coat. Set aside. Coat one of the plain cheese logs with the cranberry–pecan mixture, pressing to coat. Coat the third cheese log with the chopped pistachios, pressing with your hands to adhere. Dairy-Free Cheese Logs will keep in the refrigerator for 1 week in an airtight container. Serve cold.

Figs Stuffed with Cashew Blue Cheese

Exquisite and flavor-packed, these little morsels are a spectacular addition to any hors d'oeuvres spread. Prepare this dish when figs are in season, in early summer and early fall.

YIELD: 8 SERVINGS

8 ounces (227 g) fresh figs

1½ cups (390 g) grated or crumbled Cashew Blue Cheese (page 62)

¼ cup (60 mL) olive oil

¼ cup (60 mL) honey or maple syrup

Coarse sea salt

(1) **Prepare.** Preheat the oven to 400°F (200°C, or gas mark 6). Line a large baking sheet with parchment paper.

(2) **Stuff the figs.** Using a sharp paring knife, cut an "X" into the bottom of each fig, taking care not to slice through to the stem. Pinch the bottom of the fig so that the "X" opens slightly, then fill the opening with a tablespoon or two (15 or 20 g) of the grated Cashew Blue Cheese. Repeat with all of the figs, placing each on the prepared baking sheet as you work.

(3) **Brush and bake.** Whisk together the olive oil and honey in a small bowl. Brush this glaze onto the figs. Sprinkle with coarse sea salt and bake on the center rack of the oven for 10–12 minutes, or until the honey is just starting to caramelize. Set the pan on a wire cooling rack and let the figs cool completely on the pan.

Savory Herbed Cheese Puffs

This dairy-free take on the classic gougère takes dairy-free baking to a new level. These cheesy, herb-scented puffs are rich yet melt in the mouth.

YIELD: 40 PUFFS, 10–20 SERVINGS

½ cup (120 mL) plus 1 tablespoon (15 mL) water

½ cup (120 mL) plain unsweetened soymilk or almond milk

1 teaspoon sea salt

1 tablespoon (13 g) unrefined cane sugar

5 tablespoons (70 g) soy margarine

3 tablespoons (45 mL) coconut oil

1¼ cups (155 g) all-purpose flour

5 large eggs, lightly beaten

1 cup (260 g) grated Cashew Cheese (page 58)

Freshly ground black pepper

2 tablespoons (2 g) finely chopped fresh cilantro

2 tablespoons (8 g) finely chopped fresh parsley

2 tablespoons (6 g) finely chopped fresh chives

1 large egg, beaten, for brushing

1. **Prepare.** Preheat the oven to 400°F (200°C, or gas mark 6). Line a baking sheet with parchment paper.

2. **Make the dough.** Combine the water, soymilk, sea salt, cane sugar, margarine, and coconut oil in a small saucepan over high heat. Bring the liquid to a low boil, and then remove from the heat. Add the flour, stirring vigorously with a wooden spoon for 1–2 minutes. Return the saucepan to the heat, and continue mixing vigorously until it forms a solid dough that pulls away from the sides of the pan. Transfer the dough to a large bowl. Add the beaten eggs in several additions, stirring well with each addition until the dough is smooth.

3. **Add the cheese and herbs.** In a small bowl, mix together the grated Cashew Cheese, black pepper, and chopped herbs. Add this herbed cheese to the dough, mixing just enough to incorporate.

4. **Make the puffs.** Scoop the dough into a pastry bag, and pipe out about forty 1-inch (2.5 cm) rounds onto the prepared baking sheet, spacing the rounds 1–2 inches (3–5 cm) apart. Brush the puffs with the beaten egg. Bake for 20–30 minutes, or until golden brown and puffed up. Serve hot or at room temperature.

Savory Mini Tomato and Basil Quiches

Phyllo dough is a flaky dough that you'll find in the freezer section of your grocery. It is almost always dairy-free. If you're in a pinch for time or wish to make these quiches gluten-free, simply oil the muffin tins, bake the quiches without crusts, and serve on gluten-free dairy-free crackers.

YIELD: 24 MINI QUICHES, SERVES 12 TO 24

FOR THE PHYLLO CRUSTS:

1 box (1-pound or 0.5 kg) phyllo dough, thawed
Warm coconut oil, for brushing

FOR THE FILLING:

6 large organic eggs
1½ cups (355 mL) plain unsweetened soymilk
2 cloves garlic, finely minced
½ cup (20 g) finely chopped fresh basil
½ teaspoon sea salt
1 cup (260 g) shredded Cashew Cheese (page 58) or other dairy-free cheese
10 ounces (280 g) cherry or grape tomatoes, halved

① **Prepare.** Preheat the oven to 375°F (190°C, or gas mark 5). Lightly grease 2 standard muffin tins with coconut oil. Cut the phyllo dough into squares about 6 x 6 inches (15 x 15 cm) and place on a clean work surface.

② **Make the crust.** While working with the phyllo dough, keep the stack covered with a piece of plastic wrap and a damp kitchen towel to keep it from drying out. Brush one square with warm coconut oil, then top with another square of phyllo dough and brush with coconut oil. Fit the double-layer phyllo square into one of the muffin tins, pressing into the bottom of the cup and smoothing as much as possible. Repeat this until all 24 cups have a bottom crust. Place the tins into the oven for 5 minutes to heat, not brown.

③ **Make the filling.** Whisk the eggs very well in a large bowl. Add the soymilk, and whisk until pale yellow and well combined. Add the garlic, basil, and sea salt, whisking to incorporate. Sprinkle a little bit of the Cashew Cheese into the bottom of each phyllo cup. Top with 2 or 3 cherry tomato halves. Pour the egg–herb filling into each of the cups, filling almost to the top of the cup. Bake for 25–30 minutes, or until golden brown on top and no longer jiggly. Serve warm or cold.

Three-Onion French Onion Dip with Baked Potato Chips

Served with homemade baked potato chips and prepared with tofu and cashews, this savory, creamy classic dip gets a healthy vegan makeover.

YIELD: 6–8 SERVINGS

One 12.3-ounce (0.35 kg) block silken tofu

7 tablespoons (105 mL) extra-virgin olive oil, divided

2 tablespoons (30 mL) white wine vinegar

1 teaspoon sea salt, plus more to taste

½ teaspoon freshly ground black pepper, plus more to taste

1 cup (160 g) finely chopped yellow onion

½ cup (80 g) finely chopped shallot

½ cup (80 g) finely chopped red onion

1½ cups (345 g) Coconut Sour Cream (page 57) or store-bought dairy-free sour cream

½ teaspoon garlic powder

Chopped scallions or fresh parsley, for garnishing

Baked Potato Chips, for serving (recipe follows)

1. **Prepare the base.** Combine the tofu, 1 tablespoon (15 mL) of the olive oil, white wine vinegar, salt, and pepper in a blender. Process until smooth. While the machine is still running, drizzle in 4 tablespoons (60 mL) of olive oil until the mixture thickens. Place in the refrigerator while preparing the onions.

2. **Cook the onions.** Heat the remaining 2 tablespoons (30 mL) olive oil in a large skillet over medium heat. Add the chopped yellow onion, shallots, and red onion to the pan, cooking for 10–15 minutes, stirring often, or until the onions are lightly caramelized and very soft. Remove the pan from heat and cool the onions to completely.

3. **Make the dip.** In a medium bowl, stir together the Coconut Sour Cream, garlic powder, tofu mixture, and onions until well combined. Add salt and freshly ground pepper to taste. Cover and refrigerate for 2 hours before serving. Serve cold with Homemade Baked Potato Chips (recipe below), garnishing with scallions or fresh parsley.

BAKED POTATO CHIPS

4 large russet potatoes, sliced into thin "chips" with a sharp kitchen knife or mandolin

¼ cup (59 mL) extra-virgin olive oil

Sea salt, for sprinkling

Preheat the oven to 450°F (230°C, or gas mark 8). Toss the potato slices with the olive oil until coated and arrange on a large baking sheet in an even layer. Sprinkle with sea salt and bake until crispy and golden brown, about 20–30 minutes. (Watch them closely for their final minutes to make sure they don't burn!) Cool chips on the pan on a wire cooling rack. Serve at room temperature.

Vegan Spanakopita with Tofu Ricotta

Phyllo dough is a flaky dough that you'll find in the freezer section of your grocery. It is almost always dairy free. Although spanakopita is usually prepared with cheese fillings and tons of butter, this tofu-filled coconut-brushed version makes the savory Greek treat a little healthier, while still retaining key flavors.

YIELD: 30 TRIANGLES, 10–15 SERVINGS

1 tablespoon (15 mL) extra-virgin olive oil

2 pounds (0.9 kg) baby spinach, stems removed

One recipe Tofu Ricotta (page 63)

1 teaspoon ground nutmeg, freshly ground if possible

1 teaspoon sea salt

20 phyllo sheets, thawed if frozen

1 cup (235 mL) melted coconut oil or soy margarine

① **Prepare the pan.** Preheat the oven to 375°F (190°C, or gas mark 5). Line a large baking sheet with parchment paper.

② **Make the filling.** Heat the olive oil in a large heavy-bottomed skillet or pan over medium heat. Add the baby spinach and cook, stirring constantly for about 3–4 minutes, or until the spinach is all wilted. Remove the pan from heat and allow the spinach to cool for about 10 minutes, or until cool enough to handle. Using your hands or paper towels, squeeze any excess liquid from the spinach, then transfer to a cutting board and coarsely chop. Transfer chopped spinach to a medium bowl and add the Tofu Ricotta, nutmeg, and salt, stirring just to combine.

③ **Prepare the phyllo.** While working with the phyllo dough, keep the stack covered with a piece of plastic wrap and a damp kitchen towel to keep it from drying out. Place a piece of phyllo dough on a clean work surface with the long side of the sheet nearest to you. Brush the sheet with some of the melted coconut oil, then top with another sheet and brush with some coconut oil. Using a sharp knife or a pizza cutter, slice the phyllo into long, thin strips about 3 inches (7.5 cm) thick.

④ **Make the spanakopita.** Place 1–2 teaspoons (5–10 g) of the filling in the corner of one of the strips, then fold the corner over to the other side, forming a triangular envelope around the filling. Take the lowest point and fold this up to the opposite side, repeating this pattern until you've reached the other end of the strip (like folding a flag) and have ended with a neatly folded triangle pouch. Place the triangle seam side down on the prepared baking sheet, lightly brush with more coconut oil, and repeat until you use all of the phyllo and filling.

⑤ **Bake.** Bake the spanakopita for 20–25 minutes until golden brown. Transfer to a cooling rack to cool slightly before serving. Serve warm.

Cream of Broccoli Soup

This healthy version of the classic cream soup is an excellent way to get your greens. Each serving contains over a cup (70 g) of broccoli, which is rich in vitamin C, B vitamins including folate, and calcium. It's a creamy soup to enjoy and share with those you love.

YIELD: 8 CUPS (1.9 L), 4 SERVINGS

1 tablespoon (15 mL) extra-virgin olive oil

1 yellow onion, finely chopped

1 large russet potato, peeled and chopped

4 cups (0.9 L) low-sodium vegetable stock

¼ teaspoon sea salt, plus more to taste

¼ teaspoon freshly ground black pepper, plus more to taste

5 cups (355 g) fresh broccoli florets

½ cup (120 mL) coconut cream or soymilk

① **Sauté, simmer, and blend.** Add the oil to a Dutch oven or large stockpot over medium heat. Stir in the onion and cook until soft and translucent, about 4–6 minutes. Add the chopped potato, vegetable stock, sea salt, and black pepper, and bring to a boil. Reduce the heat to low and simmer for about 15 minutes, or until the potato is tender. Add the broccoli and cook for 3–5 minutes longer, or until the broccoli is no longer crisp but not overcooked. Transfer the soup to a blender or food processor and puree until smooth (you can also use an immersion blender to do this). Return the soup to the Dutch oven or stockpot, and stir in the coconut cream or soymilk. Season with additional sea salt and pepper to taste, and serve immediately.

Cream of Mushroom Soup

Better than any canned mushroom soup you've ever had, this three-mushroom soup is loaded with flavor and nutrients. Serve with slices of crusty bread or dairy-free crackers.

YIELD: 10 CUPS (2.3 L), 6–8 SERVINGS

Two 15-ounce (0.4 kg) cans full-fat coconut milk, refrigerated overnight

6 tablespoons (90 mL) coconut oil, divided

2 large leeks, white and light green parts only, washed well and chopped

2 large cloves garlic, minced

8 ounces (225 g) fresh cremini mushrooms, stems removed and sliced

8 ounces (225 g) fresh shitake mushrooms, stems removed and sliced

8 ounces (225 g) fresh portobello mushrooms, stems removed and sliced

1 tablespoon (2.7 g) dried thyme

3 tablespoons (22 g) all-purpose flour

1 cup (235 mL) dry white wine

6 cups (1.4 L) low-sodium vegetable stock

1 teaspoon sea salt

¼ teaspoon freshly ground black pepper

1½ cups (355 mL) unsweetened almond milk, cashew milk, or soymilk

¼ cup (15 g) finely chopped fresh parsley

Coconut cream, for garnishing (optional)

① **Prepare the coconut cream.** Puncture the refrigerated cans of coconut milk and drain the clear liquid. Open the cans and scoop the coconut cream into a small bowl. Set aside.

② **Make the soup.** Heat 3 tablespoons (45 mL) of the coconut oil in a Dutch oven or heavy-bottomed stockpot over medium-low heat. Add the leeks and garlic, and cook, stirring often, until the leeks just begin to brown slightly, about 10 minutes. Turn up the heat to medium and add the mushrooms and dried thyme. Cook for 5–10 minutes or until the mushrooms are just tender. Add the remaining 3 tablespoons (45 mL) coconut oil. Once the oil is completely melted, add the all-purpose flour, stirring vigorously for 1 minute (some flour will stick to the mushrooms—this is fine just keep stirring). Add the white wine and cook for 1 minute more, stirring constantly to prevent burning the flour. Stir in the vegetable stock, sea salt, and black pepper. Bring the soup to a boil. Turn down the heat to low and simmer for 15–20 minutes, stirring occasionally.

③ **Blend and serve.** Transfer half of the soup to a blender or food processor and blend until creamy. Return this to the rest of the soup, and stir in the reserved coconut cream and almond milk. Stir in the fresh parsley and cook until the soup is just heated through. Serve immediately, topping each bowl with a dollop of coconut cream, if desired.

Cream of Tomato Soup

This grown-up whole-food take on the dairy-laden classic is still every bit as comforting and bright. And, besides a little simmering and some blending, it's almost as easy to make.

YIELD: 6 CUPS (1.4 L), 4 SERVINGS

One 15-ounce (0.4 kg) can full-fat coconut milk, refrigerated overnight

3 tablespoons (45 mL) coconut oil

1 medium yellow onion, finely chopped

1 clove garlic, finely chopped

2 tablespoons (32 g) tomato paste

2 tablespoons (15 g) all-purpose flour

3 cups (705 mL) low-sodium vegetable broth

One 28-ounce (0.8 kg) can crushed tomatoes

2 tablespoons (26 g) organic unrefined sugar

½ teaspoon sea salt, plus more to taste

½ cup (120 mL) unsweetened soymilk or almond milk

Freshly ground black pepper, to taste

Coconut cream, for garnishing (optional)

① **Prepare the coconut cream.** Puncture the refrigerated can of coconut milk and drain the clear liquid. Open the can and scoop the coconut cream into a small bowl. Set aside.

② **Make the soup.** In a Dutch oven or stockpot, heat the coconut oil over medium heat. Add the onion and garlic and cook, stirring often, until the onion is soft and translucent. Add the tomato paste and cook for 1–2 minutes, stirring constantly. Add the flour and cook for 1 minute more, stirring constantly. Gradually add the vegetable broth, continuing to stir until all has been added. Add the crushed tomatoes, sugar, and salt and stir to incorporate. Turn down the heat to low and simmer for 30 minutes.

③ **Blend and serve.** Working in batches, transfer the soup to a blender or food processor and blend until creamy. Return the soup to the pot, and stir in the reserved coconut cream and soymilk. Season with sea salt and black pepper, and serve immediately with a dollop of coconut cream, if desired.

Creamy Potato and Leek Soup

Rustic, nutritious, and comforting, this creamy soup is wonderful on a cold day served with a slice of crusty bread.

YIELD: 10 CUPS (2.3 L), 6–8 SERVINGS

Two 15-ounce (440 mL) cans full-fat coconut milk, refrigerated overnight

3 tablespoons (45 g) olive oil or canola oil

3 large leeks, white and light green parts only, washed very well and chopped

2 celery stalks, washed well and finely chopped

¼ cup (28 g) finely grated carrot

2 large cloves garlic, minced

3 pounds (1.4 kg) red potatoes, scrubbed, peeled, and chopped

½ cup (120 mL) dry white wine

4 cups (0.9 L) low-sodium vegetable broth

1 cup (235 mL) unsweetened almond, hemp, or soymilk

2 tablespoons (30 mL) fresh lemon juice

¼ teaspoon sea salt

¼ teaspoon freshly ground black pepper

¼ cup (8 g) finely chopped fresh chives

¼ cup (15 g) finely chopped fresh parsley

① **Prepare the coconut cream.** Puncture the cans of refrigerated coconut milk, and drain out the clear liquid. Open the cans, and scoop out the coconut cream into a small dish. Set aside.

② **Sauté and simmer the vegetables.** Heat the olive oil in a 6-quart (5.5 L) Dutch oven or stockpot over medium heat. Add the leeks, celery stalks, grated carrot, and garlic. Cook, stirring occasionally, until the leeks have softened slightly. Add the potatoes and stir just to mix, then turn up the heat to medium high. Add the white wine and cook for 3–5 minutes longer, or until most of the wine has been absorbed. Add the vegetable broth, bring the soup to a boil, then turn down the heat to low and simmer the vegetables uncovered for 30–40 minutes or until the vegetables are very tender, adding water or additional broth if necessary.

③ **Finish the soup.** In a blender or food processor, blend half of the soup until very creamy, then add back to the rest of the soup. (As an alternative, use an immersion blender and just blend the soup until it is creamy but still chunky.) Add the unsweetened almond milk, stirring well to combine, followed by the reserved coconut cream and fresh lemon juice, stirring just to combine. Season with salt and pepper. Stir in the chives and parsley and serve immediately.

Chapter 11

MAIN COURSES AND SIDES

CASEROLES, PASTA DISHES, pizzas, and pies are all often prepared with butter, cheese, milk, and other dairy by the cupful. They are seldom healthy. Main dishes should be satisfying, and I've found that the way to truly satisfy an appetite is with lots of veggies and lots of variation. (And, of course, no dairy.)

These entrees are flavorful, healthier renditions of comfort food favorites that rely heavily on nutritious foods and won't leave you hungry.

Asparagus Risotto

Cooking a good risotto is all about patience and stirring. Adding ingredients in the right order and allowing the rice to absorb one addition of liquid before adding the next is paramount. But it's worth it! Arborio rice is naturally creamy, so although risottos usually call for dairy, they don't really need it. Blanching the asparagus keeps it tender-crisp and bright green and prevents overcooking.

YIELD: 4 SERVINGS

4 cups (940 mL) water

8-10 ounces (227-284 g) fresh asparagus, chopped into 2-inch (5 cm) pieces

Juice from 1 lemon

3½ cups (0.8 L) vegetable stock

2 tablespoons (30 mL) olive oil, divided

2 large cloves garlic

½ cup (80 g) finely chopped onion

1 teaspoon dried thyme

1 cup (195 g) uncooked Arborio rice

½ cup (120 mL) dry white wine

3 tablespoons (42 g) nonhydrogenated dairy-free soy margarine

¼ cup (25 g) dairy-free Parmesan

Sea salt and freshly ground black pepper, to taste

Lemon zest, for garnishing

① **Blanch the asparagus.** Bring water to boil in a small saucepan. Add the asparagus and boil for 1 minute. Drain and immediately run cold water over it to stop the cooking. Transfer to a bowl or dish and drizzle with fresh lemon juice.

② **Make the risotto.** Place the vegetable stock in a saucepan over medium-high heat. Bring to a simmer, turn down the heat to low, and cover. In another heavy-bottomed saucepan, heat 1 tablespoon (15 mL) of the olive oil over medium-high heat. Add the garlic, onions, and thyme, and cook, stirring often, until the onions are soft and fragrant, 3-6 minutes. Add the remaining 1 tablespoon (15 mL) olive oil, followed by the Arborio rice, and cook, stirring constantly, until the rice is evenly coated with the oil and starts to snap and pop. Add the wine, stirring constantly until the liquid is completely absorbed. Ladle the simmering broth into the pan, ¾ cup (175 mL) at a time, stirring constantly, and allow the rice to absorb all the liquid from one addition before adding the next. Cook until all of the broth has been added and the rice grains are solid in the middle, translucent around the edges, and creamy, about 20 minutes.

③ **Finish the risotto.** Add the asparagus and cook for 2-3 minutes more, or until the asparagus is tender but still crisp. Stir in the margarine and Parmesan. Add salt and pepper to taste and garnish with fresh lemon zest. Serve immediately.

Baked Mac n' Cheese

This healthier version of the creamy, cheesy favorite is always a hit with kids and adults alike, and as a bonus, it's easy to make and serve. Toss in 1 cup (71 g) chopped broccoli or other vegetables to add more good things to the dish.

YIELD: 6–8 SERVINGS

FOR THE MAC N' CHEESE:

1 pound (0.5 kg) elbow pasta

1 heaping cup (135 g) raw cashews

½ cup (60 g) nutritional yeast

1½ teaspoons salt

½ teaspoon onion powder

½ teaspoon garlic powder

3½ cups (0.8 L) plain unsweetened almond, cashew, or soymilk

3 tablespoons (24 g) cornstarch

½ cup (120 mL) canola oil

1 tablespoon (16 g) white miso

1 tablespoon (15 mL) lemon juice

⅓ cup (87 g) grated Cashew Cheese (page 58) or store-bought dairy-free cheese

FOR THE BREADCRUMB TOPPING:

8 thick slices day-old bread

3 tablespoons (45 mL) olive oil or soft dairy-free margarine

① **Prepare the pasta.** Preheat the oven to 325°F (160°C, or gas mark 3). Lightly oil a 9 x 13-inch (23 x 33 cm) casserole dish. Bring a medium pot of salted water to a rolling boil. Add the elbow pasta and cook according to the package's instructions until al dente. Drain.

② **Prepare the cheese sauce.** In a blender or food processor, process the cashews until finely ground but not creamy. Add the nutritional yeast, salt, onion powder, and garlic powder, and pulse just until combined. In a small saucepan, combine the dairy-free milk and cornstarch, mixing until dissolved. Add the canola oil and place over medium heat. Cook, stirring often, until the milk thickens slightly, about 5 minutes. With the blender or food processor still running, add the dairy-free milk to the ground cashew mixture, blending until creamy. Add the miso and lemon juice and blend until combined.

③ **Combine.** Toss the pasta with the cheese sauce and grated cashew cheese, and transfer to the prepared casserole dish.

④ **Prepare the breadcrumb topping, then bake.** In a food processor, pulse the bread slices until they turn into coarse crumbs. Toss the breadcrumbs with the olive oil or margarine until evenly coated. Sprinkle the topping on the macaroni and cover with foil. Bake for 40 minutes, then remove the foil and bake for 20–30 minutes longer, or until browned and bubbly. Serve hot.

Chicken in Almond Cream Sauce

The combination of almond milk and coconut cream makes this rich sauce flavorful and balanced. Feel free to add other fresh herbs you have on hand, and serve over baked sweet potatoes, pasta, rice, or vegetables.

YIELD: 4 SERVINGS

FOR THE CHICKEN:

4 organic boneless, skinless chicken breasts
1 teaspoon freshly ground black pepper
1 teaspoon salt
1 teaspoon garlic powder
All-purpose flour, for dredging (optional)
3 tablespoons (45 mL) coconut oil

FOR THE ALMOND CREAM SAUCE:

One 15-ounce (440 mL) can full-fat coconut milk, refrigerated overnight
¼ cup (60 mL) dry white wine
1 cup (235 mL) plain unsweetened almond milk
1 teaspoon fresh lemon juice
¼ cup (15 g) finely chopped fresh Italian parsley
3 tablespoons (26 g) capers, drained and rinsed
Salt and pepper, to taste

1 **Prepare the chicken breasts.** Season the chicken breasts with the black pepper, salt, and garlic powder. Rub the seasonings into the chicken on all sides. Dredge the breasts in flour to coat. Heat the coconut oil in a large skillet over medium-high heat. Add the breasts and cook, turning several times, until browned on both sides. Transfer the chicken breasts to a plate and cover with foil while preparing the sauce.

2 **Prepare the cream sauce.** Puncture the can of coconut milk and drain out the clear liquid. Open the can and scoop out the coconut cream into a small dish. Return the same skillet you used to brown the chicken to medium-high heat and add the white wine, turning the pan to coat. Cook for 1 minute or so, until most of the liquid has evaporated. Add the coconut cream, almond milk, and fresh lemon juice, and heat just until hot. Remove from the heat and add the fresh parsley and capers. Add salt and pepper to taste. Pour the cream sauce over the chicken breasts and serve immediately.

Better Eggplant Parmesan

This healthy, protein-rich entrée is great for weeknights and family dinners. Don't let the list of ingredients and steps discourage you—the dish comes together easily and quickly. Use a store-bought marinara sauce, or make the Fresh Marinara found in the Baked Homemade Ravioli with Tofu Ricotta (page 120).

YIELD: 6–8 SERVINGS

FOR THE EGGPLANTS:

Salt, for sprinkling

Two large eggplants, sliced into slices ¼-inch (6 mm) thick

Olive oil, for brushing

FOR THE BREADCRUMBS:

4 pieces toasted whole-grain bread (gluten free is fine, too)

1 teaspoon dried oregano

1 teaspoon dried thyme

Dash of salt and pepper

1 tablespoon (15 mL) olive oil

FOR THE TOFU CHEESE SAUCE:

One 12.3-ounce (0.4 kg) block extra-firm silken tofu

1 cup (235 mL) vegetable broth

½ cup (120 mL) plain almond milk, coconut milk, or hemp milk

¼ cup (30 g) nutritional yeast

3 tablespoons (45 g) tahini

1 tablespoon (15 mL) olive oil

1 teaspoon onion powder

1 teaspoon garlic powder

⅛ teaspoon salt, or to taste

2 tablespoons (16 g) cornstarch

FOR THE TOMATO BASE:

1 tablespoon (15 mL) olive oil

One medium Vidalia onion, finely chopped

4 cups (950 g) marinara sauce, store-bought or homemade (page 120)

① **Prepare the eggplants.** Lightly salt the eggplant slices, then put them on a cooling rack or colander placed over a bowl for 15–20 minutes to drain (this will prevent the eggplant from becoming soggy while cooking).

② **Make the breadcrumbs.** Place the toasted whole-grain bread slices into a food processor with the oregano, thyme, and a dash of salt and pepper. Process until crumbly and mixed well. Add the olive oil, and process once or twice more to coat. (As an alternative, prepare the breadcrumbs by hand by crumbling the bread as finely as you can, then mix in the other ingredients.)

③ **Broil the eggplant slices.** Lightly oil a large baking sheet. Rinse the eggplant slices under cold water, pat them dry with a paper towel, and transfer them to the prepared baking sheet. Brush lightly with olive oil, then place under the broiler for 2–3 minutes or until browned. Turn down the oven to 350°F (180°C, or gas mark 4).

④ **Make the cheese sauce.** Place the tofu into a blender and process until very creamy. Place the rest of the ingredients for the cheese sauce into a blender, and process until smooth.

⑤ **Make the red sauce.** Heat the olive oil in a medium saucepan over medium heat. Add the onion and cook, stirring often, until the onion is soft and translucent, 4–6 minutes. Add the marinara sauce, and heat until just warmed.

⑥ **Assemble the casserole and bake.** Lightly oil a 9 x 13-inch (23 x 33 cm) casserole dish. Place half of the eggplant slices in a single layer in the bottom of the dish. Sprinkle one-third of the breadcrumbs on top of the eggplant slices, followed by half of the marinara sauce and then half of the cheese sauce. Add the rest of the eggplant, followed by one-third of the breadcrumbs, the remaining half of the marinara sauce, and the rest of the cheese sauce. Top evenly with the remaining breadcrumbs. Bake on the center rack in the oven for 20–25 minutes or until golden brown on top. Serve hot.

Baked Homemade Ravioli with Tofu Ricotta

If making your own dough at home is too much work on a busy night, wonton wrappers make excellent ready-cut substitutes for homemade ravioli dough.

YIELD: 6–8 SERVINGS

FOR THE RAVIOLI DOUGH:

1½ cups (185 g) all-purpose flour
½ cup (60 g) whole-wheat pastry flour
Pinch of salt
3 large organic eggs
1 tablespoon (15 mL) olive oil

FOR THE TOFU RICOTTA FILLING:

2 recipes Tofu Ricotta (page 63)
¼ cup (10 g) finely chopped fresh basil
¼ cup (10 g) finely chopped fresh oregano
1 tablespoon (15 mL) extra-virgin olive oil

FOR THE FRESH MARINARA SAUCE:

3 tablespoon (45 mL) extra-virgin olive oil
¼ cup (37.5 g) minced garlic
1 medium yellow onion, finely chopped
½ cup (120 mL) dry white wine
2 tablespoons (32 g) tomato paste
¼ cup (15 g) finely chopped Italian parsley
2 tablespoon (3.4 g) dried thyme
Two 28-ounce (0.8 kg) cans crushed tomatoes
¼ cup (60 mL) vegetable stock
Salt and freshly ground black pepper

1. **Make the dough.** Sift together the flours and salt in a large bowl. Create a well in the center. Add the eggs and oil to the well and, using a fork, whisk the eggs with the oil. Begin pulling flour from the edges of the bowl into the center until the dough almost comes together. It will be stiff at this point and difficult to mix by hand. Turn out the dough onto a well-floured surface and knead for 10 minutes or until the dough is elastic, adding more olive oil if it feels dry. Cover the dough with a clean, damp kitchen towel and let it rest while making the filling and the sauce.

2. **Make the filling.** Place the Tofu Ricotta, herbs, and olive oil in a medium bowl, stirring until well mixed.

3. **Make the sauce.** Heat the olive oil in a large saucepan over medium-high heat. Add the garlic and chopped onion and cook, stirring often, until the onions are soft and fragrant, about 5 minutes. Add the white wine, and continue to cook, stirring often, until all or most of the wine has been absorbed. Add the tomato paste, parsley, and thyme, followed by the crushed tomatoes. Stir well. Add the vegetable stock, then bring the sauce to a simmer. Simmer, stirring occasionally, for 30 minutes. Season with salt and pepper.

4. **Roll out the dough.** If you are using a pasta machine or crank, divide the dough into three or four pieces, keeping those you are not using beneath the damp towel. Run each piece through several times until the pasta is smooth and very thin. If you are rolling the dough by hand, roll it out on a lightly floured surface, and when it becomes tough to work with, place it beneath a damp kitchen towel to rest for 5–10 minutes before returning to it. Keep rolling and resting it until your dough is smooth and very thin. Use a floured 2–3-inch (5–7.5 cm) ravioli stamp or cutter to cut your dough into ravioli.

5. **Prepare the pan.** Preheat the oven to 350°F (180°C, or gas mark 4). Pour half of the sauce into a large Dutch oven or casserole dish

6. **Assemble, boil, and bake.** Place 1–2 tablespoons (depending on ravioli size) of Tofu Ricotta filling in the center of half of the ravioli squares. Moisten the edges of the ravioli and, using dry hands, press the remaining ravioli halves onto the filled halves. Bring a pot of salted water to boil, and gently lower the squares into the pot for 2–3 minutes. Remove the ravioli gently with a slotted spoon and transfer them to the prepared Dutch oven. Cover the pasta with the remaining sauce and bake for 20 minutes. Serve immediately.

Buttery Chicken Pot Pie

A melt-in-your mouth wheat crust, vegetable–chicken filling, and creamy sauce make this version of the classic taste like anything but alternative. Whip this up on a cold day or when you want to bring the family together with a really special, comforting dish.

YIELD: ONE 9-INCH (23 CM) PIE, SERVES 8

FOR THE CRUST:

1¼ cups (156 g) all-purpose flour

1¼ cups (168 g) whole-wheat flour

1 teaspoon organic cane sugar

½ teaspoon salt

½ cup (112 g) nonhydrogenated soy margarine, cut into pieces and very cold

½ cup (112 g) coconut butter, at room temperature

⅓–½ cup (80–120 mL) cold water, plus more if necessary

FOR THE FILLING:

1 pound (455 g) skinless, boneless organic chicken breasts

1½ cups (195 g) sliced fresh carrots

2 stalks of celery, finely chopped

1 cup (130 g) frozen green peas

Water, for simmering

⅓ cup (80 mL) coconut oil

1 medium yellow onion, finely chopped

¼ cup (31 g) all-purpose flour

½ teaspoon salt, plus more for serving

¼ teaspoon freshly ground black pepper, plus more for serving

1 cup (235 mL) vegetable broth

2 cups (475 mL) plain unsweetened soymilk or hemp milk

① **Prepare the dough.** In a medium bowl, sift together the flours, sugar, and salt. Cut in the soy margarine and coconut butter using a pastry cutter or your hands until the mixture resembles a crumbly meal, with granules no bigger than the size of a pea. Add the cold water, 1 tablespoon (15 mL) at a time, until the dough just comes together and is not too sticky or too dry. Turn the dough out onto a lightly floured surface and knead for a minute or so until the dough comes together and is no longer sticky. Divide the dough into two pieces and wrap each tightly in plastic wrap. Chill for 30 minutes.

② **Make the crust.** Preheat the oven to 425°F (220°C, or gas mark 7). Lightly grease or oil a 9-inch (23 cm) pie plate or casserole dish. Set aside. Turn out the dough onto a lightly floured surface. Using a rolling pin, roll out half of the dough to about ⅛ inch (6 mm) thick and carefully transfer to the prepared pie plate. Fit into the pie plate and pinch together a crust around the edge of the plate with your fingers. Prick the bottom of the dough in several places with a fork and place the crust into the freezer while preparing the filling.

③ **Make the filling.** In a large saucepan over medium-high heat, combine the chicken, sliced carrots, chopped celery, and peas. Add just enough water to cover the ingredients by 1 inch (2.5 cm). Bring to a boil, turn down the heat, cover, and simmer the ingredients for 30 minutes. Remove the saucepan from the heat and drain the liquid. Transfer the chicken to a cutting board and coarsely chop. Return the chicken to the vegetables and set aside.

In another saucepan over medium-high heat, melt the coconut oil and add the chopped onions. Cook, stirring often, for 3–6 minutes, or until the onions are soft and fragrant. Add the flour, salt, and pepper and cook for 1 minute, stirring constantly to prevent burning the flour. Gradually add the vegetable broth and soy or hemp milk, stirring constantly to combine. Continue cooking and stirring until the sauce has thickened slightly.

④ **Assemble and bake.** Roll out the remaining half of the crust dough to about ⅛ inch (6 mm) thick on a lightly floured surface. Place the chicken and vegetables into the bottom crust, then pour the hot sauce on top. Immediately add the top crust and pinch around the edges to seal. Make several slits in the crust with a sharp knife to allow steam to escape. Place in the oven and bake for 35–40 minutes, or until golden brown. Serve hot.

Garlic Butter Pasta with Spinach and Mushrooms

This recipe is a go-to meal for busy weeknights. For easy plan-ahead meals, roast your garlic and combine the ingredients for the garlic butter ahead of time, then store in the refrigerator until you're ready to whip up dinner.

YIELD: 6–8 SERVINGS

FOR THE GARLIC BUTTER:

2 heads garlic

Olive oil, for roasting

1 cup (236 mL) extra-virgin coconut oil, at room temperature

3 tablespoons (23 g) nutritional yeast

3 tablespoons (7.5 g) finely chopped fresh basil

¾ teaspoon sea salt, plus more to taste

FOR THE PASTA:

1 pound (455 g) fettuccini pasta

1 small yellow onion, finely chopped

12 ounces (340 g) cremini mushrooms, washed and sliced

3 cups (90 g) fresh baby spinach, washed well and stems removed

Salt and pepper

① **Roast the garlic.** Place heads of garlic on individual pieces of foil. Drizzle each with olive oil, wrap in foil, and place in the oven for 45 minutes to 1 hour. Remove from the oven and cool until it is cool enough to touch.

② **Make the garlic butter.** Remove the cloves from the skin with your fingers (they will slide right out), dropping the soft cloves into a small bowl and discarding the skins. Add the coconut oil, nutritional yeast, basil, and sea salt, and mash together until well mixed.

③ **Make the pasta.** Bring a large pot of salted water to a rolling boil. Add the pasta and cook according to the manufacturer's instructions. Drain. In a large skillet over medium-high heat, add ¼ cup (60 g) of the garlic butter. Add the onion and cook until just softened, 3–4 minutes. Add the mushrooms and cook until lightly browned, about 4 more minutes. Add the pasta, spinach, and remaining garlic butter, and toss to combine. (If your skillet isn't big enough, toss everything together in a large serving bowl.) Season to taste with salt and pepper. Serve immediately.

Herbed Mushroom Bread Pudding

Somewhere between a savory French toast casserole and a stuffing, this dish makes a nice vegetarian side for Thanksgiving celebrations, family dinners, and brunches.

YIELD: ONE 9 X 13-INCH (23 X 33 CM) CASSEROLE, 8 SERVINGS

2 large sweet potatoes

One 1-pound (455 g) loaf of challah bread, cut into 1-inch (2.5 cm) cubes

¼ cup (60 mL) extra-virgin olive oil

2 tablespoons (5.4 g) dried thyme

⅛ teaspoon salt

3 tablespoons (45 g) coconut oil

1 small yellow onion, finely chopped

1 cup (70 g) sliced cremini mushrooms

1 cup (70 g) sliced portobello mushrooms

1 cup (70 g) sliced shiitake mushrooms, stemmed

1 cup (120 g) finely chopped celery (2–3 large stalks)

¼ cup (15 g) finely chopped fresh parsley

¼ cup (13 g) finely chopped fresh rosemary

¼ cup (13 g) finely chopped fresh oregano

3 cups (705 mL) almond milk or cashew milk

9 large organic eggs, lightly beaten

2 teaspoons (12 g) salt

3 tablespoons (23 g) nutritional yeast

① **Bake the sweet potato and toast the bread cubes.** Preheat the oven to 400°F (200°C, or gas mark 6). Wrap the sweet potatoes in foil and bake for 1 hour or until very soft. Once cool enough to handle, remove the skins and chop the potatoes into 1-inch (2.5 cm) chunks.

Combine the bread cubes with the olive oil, thyme, and salt in a large bowl, tossing well to coat. Spread the cubes out onto a large baking sheet and toast for 10–15 minutes, or until just golden. Cool the cubes slightly, then return to the large bowl. Turn down the heat to 350°F (180°C, or gas mark 4). Lightly oil a 9 x 13-inch (23 x 33 cm) casserole dish.

② **Prepare the vegetables.** In a large skillet, heat the coconut oil over medium-high heat. Add the chopped onion, mushrooms, and celery. Cook, stirring often, until the vegetables are soft and most of the liquid has evaporated, about 10 minutes. Add to the bread cubes along with the fresh herbs and chopped sweet potato, stirring just to combine.

③ **Make the custard, assemble, and bake.** In another bowl, whisk together the almond milk with the eggs, salt, and nutritional yeast. Pour into the bowl with the bread and vegetables, then transfer to the prepared casserole dish. Bake uncovered for 1 hour, or until puffed and golden brown. Cool the bread pudding for 10–15 minutes before serving.

Lighter Enchiladas in Cashew Cheese Sauce

This casserole is satisfying, nutritious, and full of spice and flavor. This dish can be prepared ahead of time and frozen. Prepare everything but the Cashew Cheese Dip, and when it's time to cook your enchiladas, remove from the freezer, top with freshly made Cashew Cheese Dip, and bake covered for 30 minutes, then uncovered for 15 minutes.

YIELD: 8 SERVINGS

FOR THE FILLING:

3 large sweet potatoes

1 tablespoon (15 mL) olive oil

1 cup (160 g) finely chopped yellow onion

2 cloves garlic, finely chopped

2 fresh jalapeño peppers, stems, seeds, and membranes removed, finely minced

2 cups (60 g) baby spinach, stems removed

One 15-ounce (0.4 kg) can organic black beans, drained and rinsed

¼ cup (4 g) finely chopped fresh cilantro

2 tablespoons (28 g) canned chipotles in adobo

FOR ASSEMBLING:

Sixteen 6-inch (15 cm) corn tortillas

Cilantro and chopped scallion, for garnishing

FOR THE CASHEW CHEESE SAUCE:

1 recipe Cashew Cheese Dip (page 94)

① **Prepare the filling.** Preheat the oven to 400°F (200°C, or gas mark 6). Wrap the sweet potatoes in foil and bake until soft, about 1 hour. Once cool enough to handle, remove the skins and roughly chop the potatoes (it's okay if they're mushy).

Meanwhile, in a large skillet over medium-high heat, heat the olive oil. Add the yellow onion and garlic, and cook, stirring often, for 3-5 minutes, or until the onions soften. Add the jalapeño peppers and cook for 2 minutes longer. Remove the skillet from the heat and add the spinach, black beans, cilantro, and adobo, stirring just to combine. Transfer the filling to a large bowl and fold in the sweet potato with a spatula or spoon.

② **Prepare the tortillas.** Stack the tortillas, wrap in foil, and place in the oven for 5-10 minutes. This will make them softer and easier to work with while assembling.

③ **Assemble the enchiladas.** Lightly oil a 9 x 13-inch (23 x 33 cm) casserole dish. Spoon about 1 cup (260 g) of the Cashew Cheese Dip into the bottom of the dish. Place about ⅓ cup (80 g) of the filling onto the center of each tortilla, then roll each tightly and place seam side down in the casserole dish. Pour the remaining Cashew Cheese Dip over the top of the enchiladas and bake, uncovered, for 15-20 minutes, or until golden and bubbly. Garnish with cilantro and chopped scallions and serve hot.

Savory Buckwheat Tomato Crepes

Making perfect crepes is easy once you learn the rhythm of crepe making, which comes from practice. Crepes should spread very easily onto the bottom of the pan and cook in under 2 minutes, so your pan needs to be the correct temperature, which usually takes a few adjustments to get right. If your first few crepes bite the dust, don't panic—just adjust until your pan is the correct temperature and you have the pan-swirling action down.

YIELD: 4 SERVINGS

FOR THE BUCKWHEAT CREPES:

2 cups (475 mL) cashew milk, coconut milk, or soymilk, at room temperature

1 tablespoon (12 g) organic unrefined sugar

¼ teaspoon sea salt

3 tablespoons (45 mL) melted nonhydrogenated margarine or extra-virgin olive oil

½ cup (60 g) buckwheat flour

¾ cup (93 g) all-purpose flour

4 large eggs

Coconut oil, for cooking crepes

FOR THE ROASTED TOMATO FILLING:

3 tablespoons (45 mL) olive oil

¼ cup (13 g) fresh thyme

¼ cup (10 g) finely chopped fresh basil

3 large bell peppers, preferably one of each color

1 pound (455 g) fresh tomatoes, stems removed and slice in half horizontally

1. **Prepare the crepe batter.** Place all of the crepe ingredients into a blender or food processor, and process until smooth. Transfer into a bowl or pitcher, cover, and refrigerate overnight.

2. **Preheat the oven to 400°F (200°C, or gas mark 6).** Let the crepe batter sit at room temperature while preparing the filling.

3. **Prepare the filling.** Pour the olive oil, thyme, and fresh basil into a 9 x 13 inch (23 x 33 cm) casserole dish. Add the peppers to the dish, turning in the oil and seasonings to lightly coat. Add the tomato halves and toss in the olive oil and herbs, then place cut side down in the dish. Place in the oven for 30-40 minutes, turning the peppers every 10 minutes or so. Once the peppers are puffed and browned, but not blackened, and the tomatoes are wrinkly and very soft, remove from the oven.

   Cool the vegetables enough so you can remove their skins. Hold the peppers over the baking dish with the tomatoes, then slice in half and remove the stems, seeds, and membranes. Coarsely chop the peppers and the tomatoes, and mix well. Cover with foil to keep warm while preparing the crepes.

4. **Make the crepes.** Lightly grease an 8-inch (20 cm) skillet or crepe pan with coconut oil, and place over medium-high heat. Once hot, add the crepe batter, ¼ cup (60 mL) at a time, and swirl the pan to coat with the batter. After about 1 minute (watch closely), run a heat-proof spatula around the edge of the crepe to loosen it, and then flip the crepe over to cook the other side for about 30 seconds more. Repeat until all of the batter has been used.

5. **Serve.** Place ⅓ to ½ cup (80 to 120 mL) of the filling onto each crepe, then fold over and serve immediately. Wrap any leftover crepes in plastic wrap once cool and then foil, and freeze for up to two months.

Quinoa-Crusted Cheese Pizza

This no-yeast, dairy-free, gluten-free, vegan pizza is one of the easiest you'll make—it just takes a little bit of prep time beforehand.

YIELD: ONE 12-INCH (30 CM) PIZZA, 2–4 SERVINGS

FOR THE QUINOA CRUST:

1 cup (173 g) quinoa

Water, for soaking

½ cup (80 g) cooked brown rice

½ cup (120 mL) water, plus more if needed

2 tablespoons (30 mL) oil

½–¾ teaspoon sea salt

½ teaspoon dried oregano

½ teaspoon garlic powder

FOR THE TOPPING:

1 cup (135 g) finely ground cashews

½ cup (120 mL) unsweetened almond milk

2 teaspoons (10 mL) lemon juice

3 tablespoons (23 g) nutritional yeast

½ teaspoon onion powder

½ teaspoon sea salt, or to taste

½–¾ cup (120–200 g) pizza sauce, either store-bought or homemade (recipe follows)

1 cup (260 g) grated Cashew Cheese (page 58) or other shredded dairy-free cheese

1. **Soak the quinoa.** Place the quinoa in a small bowl just big enough to fit. Add water just to cover and soak for 8 hours or overnight.

2. **Make the crust.** Preheat the oven to 450°F (230°C, or gas mark 8) and lightly oil a 12-inch (30 cm) cast-iron skillet. Drain the soaking water from the quinoa and discard. Transfer the quinoa to a blender, along with the cooked brown rice, ½ cup (120 mL) water, oil, sea salt, dried oregano, and garlic powder. Blend until the batter is thick and, for the most part, smooth. Pour the batter into the oiled skillet, using a spatula to even it out. Bake for 10 minutes, flip, and bake the other side for 5–10 minutes, or until both sides are lightly crisp and golden brown.

3. **Meanwhile, make the topping.** Combine the ground cashews, almond milk, lemon juice, nutritional yeast, onion powder, and salt in a blender, blending until smooth. Transfer to a small saucepan over medium heat and cook for about 10 minutes, stirring often, or until thickened. Set aside.

4. **Assemble the pizza.** While the crust is still hot, spread the pizza sauce evenly over the top of the crust. Sprinkle the grated Cashew Cheese over the pizza sauce, then drizzle the cheese sauce over the top. Place the skillet back in the oven for 5 minutes. Serve immediately.

SUPER-QUICK FRESH PIZZA SAUCE

YIELD: 3½ CUPS (790 G) SAUCE

Two 15-ounce (0.4 kg) cans tomato sauce
One 6-ounce (170 g) can tomato paste
1 tablespoon (3 g) dried oregano
1 teaspoon fennel seed
1 teaspoon garlic powder
1 teaspoon onion powder
1 teaspoon organic unrefined cane sugar
¼ teaspoon sea salt, or to taste

Place all the ingredients in a medium saucepan over medium heat, and stir well to combine. Bring to a boil, then turn down the heat to low and simmer, covered, for 20–30 minutes. Cool for 10 minutes, then use immediately or allow the sauce to cool completely and save for a future use. Pizza sauce will keep in an airtight container in the refrigerator for 4–5 days.

Savory Spinach–Broccoli Pie

Crumbled tofu, organic eggs, and Cashew Cheese make this savory pie a satisfying protein-rich meal. With a whole pound of spinach, this is a nutrient-rich dish that's packed with flavor.

YIELD: ONE 9-INCH (23 CM) PIE, 8 SERVINGS

FOR THE CRUST:

1 cup (125 g) all-purpose flour

½ cup (62 g) whole-wheat pastry flour

1 tablespoon (13 g) organic unrefined cane sugar

½ teaspoon salt

½ cup (120 mL) coconut oil, at room temperature

¼ cup (60 mL) water, at room temperature,
   plus more as needed

FOR THE FILLING:

2 tablespoons (30 mL) extra-virgin olive oil

1 cup (160 g) finely chopped onion

¼ cup (38 g) minced garlic

1½ pounds (0.7 kg) fresh baby spinach,
   washed well and patted dry

1 cup (70 g) fresh broccoli florets

½ cup (50 g) sliced pitted black olives

4 large organic eggs, lightly beaten

¾ cup (174 mL) almond milk or soymilk

¾ teaspoon sea salt, plus more for serving

1 cup (240 g) crumbled tofu

½ cup (130 g) shredded Cashew Cheese
   (page 58)

① **Prepare the crust.** Combine the flours, sugar, and salt in a bowl. Using a pastry cutter or your fingers, cut in the coconut oil until the mixture comes together into very soft crumbs. Add the water and stir until the soft dough comes together, adding more water 1 tablespoon (15 mL) at a time as needed. Press the dough into a disk and wrap tightly with plastic wrap. Chill for 15 minutes.

② **Roll out the dough.** (If your dough has been in the refrigerator for longer than 15 minutes, let the dough rest at room temperature for several minutes before rolling it out.) Lightly grease a 9-inch (23 cm) pie plate with coconut oil. Turn the dough out onto a lightly floured surface and roll out into a large circle about ⅛ inch (6 mm) thick. Carefully transfer to the pie plate. Pinch and tuck the dough around the edges to create a crust. Place the pie plate in the refrigerator while preparing the filling.

③ **Make the filling.** Preheat the oven to 375°F (190°C, or gas mark 5). Place the olive oil in a medium heavy-bottomed skillet over medium heat. Add the onion, and sauté until soft, about 4–6 minutes. Add the garlic and cook for 2 minutes longer, stirring constantly. Add the spinach in batches, allowing one batch to wilt completely before adding the next batch, until all has been added. Add the broccoli florets and olives, stir, and set aside to cool slightly. In a large bowl, whisk the eggs with the almond milk and sea salt. Stir in the crumbled tofu and Cashew Cheese, then add the spinach mixture and stir until combined.

④ **Bake.** Pour into the prepared crust and bake for 50 minutes to 1 hour, or until the center is no longer jiggly and the top is golden brown. Let the pie cool for 10–15 minutes before serving. Serve hot.

Stuffed Cheese and Spinach Pasta Shells

For busy weeks prepare these delectable shells a couple of days ahead of time—just fill the shells, place in the casserole dish, and freeze until you're ready to bake. Before baking, let the shells come to room temperature, then cover with the sauce and pop the dish in the oven.

YIELD: 4 SERVINGS

FOR THE SIMPLE RED SAUCE:

¼ cup (60 mL) extra-virgin olive oil

½ cup (80 g) finely chopped onion

3 large cloves garlic, minced

Two 28-ounce (0.8 kg) cans crushed tomatoes

1 tablespoon (3 g) fresh oregano, finely chopped

Salt, to taste

Red pepper flakes (optional)

FOR THE TOFU-SPINACH FILLING:

2 cups (80 g) fresh basil leaves

¾ cup (100 g) raw pine nuts

2 large cloves fresh garlic

1 tablespoon (8 g) nutritional yeast

¼ teaspoon sea salt, plus more to taste

¼ cup (60 mL) extra-virgin olive oil, as needed

One 1-pound (455 g) block of extra-firm tofu, crumbled

One 10-ounce (280 g) package frozen spinach, thawed and excess liquid pressed out

1 cup (260 g) shredded Cashew Cheese (page 58)

FOR THE PASTA:

One 16-ounce (455 g) package jumbo pasta shells (about 30 shells)

① **Prepare.** Preheat the oven to 350°F (180°C, or gas mark 4). Lightly oil a 9 x 13-inch (23 x 33 cm) casserole dish.

② **Make the sauce.** Heat the olive oil in a skillet over medium-high heat. Add the onions and sauté for 3–5 minutes, or until just soft. Add the garlic and cook for 1 minute more, stirring often so it doesn't burn. Add the crushed tomatoes and oregano and bring to a simmer for 5 minutes. Add salt to taste and a shake of red pepper flakes, if desired. Pour about 1–1½ cups (245–370 g) of the sauce in the bottom of the prepared casserole dish.

③ **Prepare the filling.** Place the basil, pine nuts, garlic, nutritional yeast, and salt in a blender or food processor. Process until the mixture is crumbly but not entirely pureed. While the machine is running, add the olive oil until the mixture comes together to form a runny paste. Place the crumbed tofu in a bowl with the pressed spinach and grated Cashew Cheese. Add half of the basil paste, and mix to combine.

④ **Boil the pasta, then fill the shells.** Bring a large pot of salted water to a rolling boil, add the shells, and cook according to the manufacturer's instructions until al dente. (Overcooked shells will tear as you attempt to fill them.) Drain and cool for several minutes until cool enough to handle. Fill each shell with the filling, placing them seam side up in a single layer in the prepared pan. Drizzle the remaining half of the basil–pine nut mixture over the shells, then ladle the remaining sauce over the shells. Cover with foil and bake for 30 minutes, then uncover and bake for an additional 15 minutes, or until bubbly. Serve hot.

Vegetable Lasagna with Tofu Ricotta

Tofu Ricotta and a cashew-based cheese sauce make this cheesy favorite healthier but every bit as delicious. Add other vegetables as you wish—thin slices of eggplant and summer squashes like zucchini can even stand in for noodles if you're feeling adventurous.

YIELD: ONE 9 X 13-INCH (23 X 33 CM) CASSEROLE, 8 SERVINGS

FOR THE CASHEW CHEESE SAUCE:

1 heaping cup (135 g) raw cashews

½ cup (60 g) nutritional yeast

1½ teaspoons salt

½ teaspoon onion powder

½ teaspoon garlic powder

3½ cups (0.8 L) plain unsweetened almond or soymilk, divided

3 tablespoons (24 g) cornstarch

½ cup (120 mL) extra-virgin olive oil

1 tablespoon (16 g) white miso

1 tablespoon (15 mL) lemon juice

FOR THE PASTA:

8 ounces (225 g) lasagna noodles

FOR THE TOFU RICOTTA FILLING:

1 tablespoon (15 mL) extra-virgin olive oil

10 ounces (284 g) cremini mushrooms, sliced

4 cups (920 g) Tofu Ricotta (page 63)

2 large organic eggs, lightly beaten

¼ cup (10 g) finely chopped fresh basil

Two 10-ounce (280 g) packages frozen spinach, defrosted and squeezed of excess moisture

6 cups (1.6 kg) marinara sauce, store-bought or homemade (page 120)

① **Prepare.** Preheat the oven to 400°F (200°C, or gas mark 6). Lightly grease a 9 x 13-inch (23 x 33 cm) casserole dish.

② **Make the cheese sauce.** Blend the cashews until finely ground but not creamy. Add the nutritional yeast, salt, onion powder, and garlic powder, and pulse just until combined. In a small saucepan, combine the dairy-free milk and cornstarch, mixing until dissolved. Add the canola oil and place over medium heat. Cook, stirring often, until the sauce thickens slightly, about 3–5 minutes. Add the sauce to the ground cashews, blending until creamy. Add the miso and lemon juice and blend.

③ **Boil the pasta.** Bring a large pot of salted water to a rolling boil and add the pasta. Cook until al dente. Drain and rinse with cold water.

④ **Meanwhile, prepare the filling.** Heat the olive oil in a saucepan or skillet over medium heat. Add the mushrooms and cook for 3–4 minutes, until just lightly browned and tender. In a small bowl, whisk together the Tofu Ricotta, eggs, and fresh basil. Stir in the spinach and sautéed mushrooms.

⑤ **Assemble and bake.** Pour about 1 cup (245 g) of the marinara sauce in the bottom of the prepared casserole dish. Arrange one layer of noodles on top. Spread one-third of the filling on top of the noodles, followed by another cup of marinara sauce and one-third of the cheese sauce. Repeat layers twice more, ending with the marinara and cheese sauce on top. Cover the dish with foil and bake for 20 minutes. Remove the foil and bake 25 more minutes, or until golden and bubbly. Cool the lasagna slightly before serving.

Spinach Fettuccine Alfredo

A fast, creamy treat, this entree will become a staple in your home. Feel free to add other vegetables such as steamed broccoli or sun-dried tomatoes to your dish for even more nutrition.

YIELD: 4–6 SERVINGS

1 pound (455 g) fettuccine pasta

4 cups (120 g) fresh baby spinach, stems removed

1 cup (95 g) finely ground cashews

2½ cups (570 mL) plain unsweetened soymilk or almond milk

½ cup (115 g) Cashew Sour Cream (page 57) or Coconut Sour Cream (page 57)

¼ cup (30 g) nutritional yeast

½ teaspoon garlic powder

¼ teaspoon sea salt, plus more to taste

Freshly ground pepper, plus more to taste

① **Cook the pasta.** Bring a large pot of salted water to a rolling boil and add the pasta. Cook until al dente according to the manufacture's instructions. Drain.

② **Prepare the spinach.** Wash the spinach well in cold water. Pat dry with paper towels, pressing out any excess liquid.

③ **Make the sauce.** In a blender or food processor, combine the ground cashews, soymilk, Cashew Sour Cream, nutritional yeast, garlic powder, and sea salt. Blend until creamy. Transfer to a small saucepan over medium heat, and cook until warmed through. Add the spinach, and cook until the spinach is wilted and bright green, stirring well to incorporate. Add the pasta, toss to coat, and serve immediately with salt and freshly ground pepper to taste.

Vegetable Pizza with Vegan Basil Pesto

This pizza is great with a sprinkling of Cashew Cheese, but it's also delicious without any cheese substitute at all! Loaded with vegetables, flavor, and nutrients, this pizza is way better than delivery.

YIELD: 4 SERVINGS

FOR THE PIZZA CRUST:

1½ cups (355 mL) warm water

One ¼-ounce (7.5 g) package active dry yeast

1 tablespoon (13 g) sugar

1 teaspoon extra virgin olive oil

1 teaspoon sea salt

2½ cups (315 g) whole-wheat flour

½ cup (60 g) all-purpose flour

FOR THE VEGAN BASIL PESTO:

2 cups (80 g) fresh basil

¾ cup (99 g) raw pine nuts

2 large cloves garlic

1 tablespoon (8 g) nutritional yeast

¼ teaspoon sea salt, plus more to taste

¼ cup (60 mL) extra-virgin olive oil, as needed

FOR THE VEGETABLE TOPPING:

1 cup (260 g) grated Cashew Cheese (page 58) (optional)

2 cups (360 g) ripe cherry tomatoes, halved

1 cup (70 g) sliced cremini mushrooms

1 green bell pepper, cored, seeded and sliced

1 cup (71 g) fresh broccoli florets

One 14-ounce (397 g) can artichoke hearts, drained and chopped

① **Prepare the crust.** In a large bowl gently combine the warm water, yeast, and sugar. Add the olive oil, salt, and whole-wheat flour. Mix until combined, then gradually add the all-purpose flour until the dough comes together and pulls away from the sides of the bowl. Turn the dough out onto a lightly floured surface and knead for 4–5 minutes, or until elastic. Place the dough in a lightly oiled bowl in a warm place, cover with a kitchen towel, and let rise for 1 hour. Punch down the dough and turn out onto a clean work surface. Knead the dough briefly into a tight ball, return the dough to the oiled bowl, and allow the dough to rise for another 45 minutes.

② **Prepare the pan.** Preheat the oven to 425°F (220°C, or gas mark 7). Lightly oil a pizza pan or baking sheet.

③ **Make the Vegan Basil Pesto.** Place the basil, pine nuts, garlic, nutritional yeast, and salt into a food processor or blender. Process until crumbly. With the machine still running, add the oil in a steady stream until the sauce becomes a spreadable paste, adding more oil as needed.

④ **Roll out the dough, assemble the pizza, and bake.** Roll out the dough into a circle about ⅛ – ¼ inch (3 to 6 mm) thick. Spread the pesto evenly over the dough, then sprinkle the Cashew Cheese on top, if using. Top with the cherry tomatoes, mushrooms, pepper, broccoli, and artichoke. Bake for 15–20 minutes, or until the crust is golden brown. Slice and serve immediately.

Best Egg Salad Ever

I'm picky about egg salad. Too much mayo ruins the dish, as does overcooking the eggs or leaving out the scallions. (Most recipes for egg salad do not include scallions, but to me, they are a must.) Of all the egg salads I've tried and made, this is the best. Serve it with crusty bread as a sandwich or over greens as a salad.

YIELD: 4 SERVINGS AS A SANDWICH FILLING

8 large organic eggs

Water, for boiling and chilling

3 tablespoons (42 g) mayonnaise, either soy or regular, store-bought or homemade (page 138)

¼ cup (60 g) plain unsweetened almond yogurt, store-bought or homemade (page 64)

1 teaspoon lemon juice

½ teaspoon curry powder

⅛ teaspoon sea salt, plus more to taste

1 large celery stalk, washed well and finely sliced

¼ cup (25 g) finely chopped fresh scallion

¼ cup (4 g) finely chopped fresh cilantro

Freshly ground black pepper, to taste

1. **Hard-boil the eggs.** Place several cups of ice water in a medium bowl. Place the eggs in a small pot just large enough to fit them in a single layer. Cover the eggs with cold water to cover by 1 inch (2.5 cm), and bring to a boil over medium-high heat. Allow the eggs to boil for 1 minute, then cover, turn off the heat, and allow the eggs to sit for 7 minutes. Transfer the eggs to the ice water for a few minutes to stop the cooking.

2. **Make the salad.** Peel and coarsely chop each egg, and transfer to a bowl. Add the mayonnaise, almond yogurt, lemon juice, curry powder, and sea salt, mixing well and mashing slightly. (The filling should still be lumpy.) Stir in the chopped celery, scallions, and cilantro until well incorporated. Add sea salt and freshly ground pepper to taste. Serve cold.

Creamy Coleslaw with Tofu Mayo

A vegan version of the picnic favorite, this creamy coleslaw is also healthier, prepared with tofu and cashews in place of conventional mayo and dairy, but so good, you'd never know.

YIELD: 6-8 SERVINGS AS A SIDE DISH

FOR THE TOFU MAYO:

One 12.3-ounce (0.3 kg) block silken tofu

5 tablespoons (75 mL) extra-virgin olive oil

2 tablespoons (30 mL) white wine vinegar

1 teaspoon sea salt, plus more to taste

FOR THE COCONUT COLESLAW:

2 tablespoons (22 g) Dijon mustard

2 tablespoons (30 mL) apple cider vinegar

1 tablespoon (15 mL) fresh lemon juice

¼ cup (50 g) granulated sugar

1 teaspoon sea salt, plus more to taste

½ cup (115 g) Coconut Sour Cream (page 57)

2 green cabbages (2½–3 pounds [1–1.3 kg]), finely shredded

2 cups (220 g) grated carrot

½ cup (80 g) grated red onion

① **Prepare the Tofu Mayo.** Place the tofu, water and all, in a blender or food processor and process on high until smooth and creamy. Add 1 tablespoon (15 mL) of the olive oil, the vinegar, and the sea salt, and process until smooth. With the blender or food processor still running, add the remaining 4 tablespoons (60 mL) olive oil in a steady stream until the mayo comes together and is thick and creamy.

② **Make the slaw.** Transfer the Tofu Mayo to a large bowl, and stir in the Dijon mustard, cider vinegar, lemon juice, sugar, sea salt, and Coconut Sour Cream. Add the shredded cabbage, grated carrot, and grated onion, and mix thoroughly. Chill for 4 hours or overnight, until the cabbage softens. Serve cold.

Garlic and Chive Mashed Potatoes

Coconut cream makes these mashed potatoes as creamy as butter-and-sour-cream potatoes, and garlic and chives give them a flavorful, colorful kick.

YIELD: 10–12 SERVINGS

Two 15-ounce (440 mL) cans full-fat coconut milk, refrigerated overnight

4 pounds (1.8 kg) russet potatoes, peeled and diced

1 tablespoon (18 g) sea salt, plus more to taste

Water, for boiling

½ cup (75 g) finely minced fresh garlic

½ cup (18 g) finely chopped fresh chives

Freshly ground black pepper, for serving

Coconut Sour Cream (page 57), for serving (optional)

① **Prepare the coconut cream.** Puncture the coconut milk cans and drain out the liquid. Open the cans and scoop out the coconut cream into a small dish.

② **Boil the potatoes.** Place the potatoes and sea salt in a large stockpot with just enough water to cover by about 2 inches (5 cm). Place over medium-high heat and bring to a boil, reduce the heat to medium-low, and cook the potatoes at a low boil for 15–20 minutes, or until very tender. Drain the potatoes and remove from the heat.

③ **Mash them.** Place the minced garlic and the coconut cream in a small saucepan. Heat over medium heat until just warmed through, then add to the potatoes. Using a potato masher or the back of a large spoon, mash the potatoes very well until creamy. Add the chives, and mix just to incorporate. Add salt to taste. Serve immediately with freshly ground black pepper and Coconut Sour Cream, if using.

Buttermilk Dinner Rolls

Pillowy, slightly sour dinner rolls are a treat for any supper. To make this recipe vegan, omit the egg wash and brush the rolls with soymilk or almond milk before baking.

YIELD: 12 GIANT ROLLS

2 cups (475 mL) plus 2 tablespoons (30 mL) soymilk, warm

2 tablespoons (30 mL) lemon juice

1 tablespoon (15 mL) melted coconut oil, plus more for serving

One ¼-ounce (7 g) package active dry yeast

2 tablespoons (40 g) honey or agave nectar

5½–6 cups (688–750 g) all-purpose flour

1 tablespoon (18 g) sea salt

1 large egg

① **Make the soy buttermilk.** In a small bowl or dish, whisk together the warm soymilk, lemon juice, and melted coconut oil until well combined.

② **Make the dough.** In a large bowl or the bowl of a stand mixer, combine the buttermilk, yeast, honey or agave, and half the flour. Mix until combined, then add the salt and the remaining half of the flour, ½ cup (60 g) at a time, until the dough pulls away from the sides of the bowl and is neither sticky nor dry. Knead on a lightly floured work surface until elastic, then return the bread to the bowl, cover with a kitchen towel, and let rise for 3 hours, or until doubled.

③ **Prepare the pan.** Lightly oil a 10-inch (25 cm) springform pan.

④ **Make the rolls.** Divide the dough into 12 equal parts. On a clean work surface, roll each part into a tight ball, placing each into the springform pan as you work. Cover the pan with a kitchen towel and let the dough rise for 1 more hour in a warm place.

⑤ **Bake.** Preheat the oven to 375°F (190°C, or gas mark 5). Whisk the egg well in a small bowl. Brush the egg over the rolls. Bake for 40–45 minutes, or until golden brown. Cool rolls in the pan for 5–10 minutes before serving, and brush lightly with coconut oil if desired. Serve warm in the pan and let guests pull their dough from the bunch.

Green Bean Casserole

The only can in this green bean casserole is the one you'll use to make your coconut cream, which you do by simply draining the liquid from a can of coconut milk and then scooping out the remaining cream. Fresh green beans, a homemade mushroom cream sauce, and baked onion rings instead of fried all make for a healthier dairy-free version of the favorite casserole.

YIELD: 6–8 SERVINGS

FOR THE BAKED ONION RINGS:

2 cups (250 g) all-purpose flour

1 tablespoon (18 g) plus 2 teaspoons (12 g) salt, divided

4 large eggs, beaten well

¼ cup (60 mL) unsweetened almond milk or soymilk

2½ cups (290 g) panko breadcrumbs

¼ cup (60 mL) olive oil

2 medium sweet yellow onions, sliced into rings and separated

FOR THE CASSEROLE:

4 cups (400 g) fresh green beans, sliced

5 cups (1.2 L) vegetable broth

¼ cup (60 mL) coconut oil

½ cup (80 g) diced onions

1 cup (70 g) sliced cremini mushrooms

3 tablespoons (24 g) all-purpose flour

4 cups (0.9 L) unsweetened almond milk or soymilk, plus more as needed

½ teaspoon sea salt, plus more to taste

½ cup (120 mL) coconut cream

① **Prepare the pan.** Preheat the oven to 450°F (230°C, or gas mark 8). Line 2 baking sheets with parchment paper.

② **Prepare the onion rings.** Set out three small bowls. In one bowl, combine the flour and 1 tablespoon (18 g) salt. In another bowl, combine the eggs and almond milk, whisking to combine. In the third bowl, combine the panko breadcrumbs, olive oil, and remaining 2 teaspoons (12 g) salt. Working with one onion ring at a time, dredge first in the flour mixture, then dip into the egg mixture, then dredge in the panko mixture. Place on the prepared baking sheet and repeat until all of the onions are coated. Bake until golden brown, 15–20 minutes.

③ **Prepare the casserole.** Turn down the heat to 350°F (180°C, or gas mark 4). Lightly grease a 2-quart (1.9 L) casserole dish. In a large stockpot or saucepan, combine the vegetable broth and green beans and bring to a boil. Boil for 8–10 minutes, or until slightly tender. Drain. Add the coconut oil to a large heavy-bottomed skillet over medium heat. Add the diced onions and cook, stirring often, until the onions are just soft, about 4–6 minutes. Add the mushrooms and cook until lightly browned and tender, about 3–4 minutes more. Add the flour and cook for 1 minute, stirring vigorously to avoid burning the flour. Gradually add the almond milk, continuing to stir constantly. Add the sea salt. Add the green beans, coconut cream, and half of the onion rings.

④ **Bake.** Pour the mixture into the prepared casserole dish. Bake for 20 minutes, then top with the remaining half of the onion rings and bake for 10 minutes more, until bubbly.

Potatoes Au Gratin

Potatoes are baked in a creamy soymilk sauce beneath a layer of homemade breadcrumbs in this dairy-free, vegan take on the classic side.

YIELD: 4-6 SERVINGS

FOR THE POTATO AND ONION LAYERS:

6 russet potatoes (about 2-3 pounds [0.9-1.3 kg]), scrubbed well and sliced into ¼-inch (6 mm) slices

1 large yellow onion, sliced into rings

Freshly ground pepper and sea salt

FOR THE CREAM SAUCE:

¼ cup (60 mL) nonhydrogenated soy margarine or coconut oil

3 tablespoons (24 g) all-purpose flour

2 cups (475 mL) plain unsweetened soymilk or almond milk

½ teaspoon sea salt, plus more to taste

1 cup (260 g) grated Cashew Cheese (page 58) or other dairy-free cheese

FOR THE BREADCRUMBS:

4 pieces toasted whole-grain bread

1 tablespoon (15 mL) olive oil

1 teaspoon dried oregano

½ teaspoon dried thyme

½ teaspoon sea salt

① **Layer the potatoes.** Preheat the oven to 375°F (190°C, or gas mark 5). Lightly grease a 1½-quart (1.4 L) casserole dish. Layer half of the potato slices in the bottom of the dish, followed by a layer of the onion, followed by the remaining potato slices. Season with freshly ground pepper and a little bit of sea salt.

② **Make the cream sauce.** Add the soy margarine or coconut oil to a heavy-bottom saucepan over medium heat. Add the flour, and cook for 1 minute, stirring constantly to prevent burning the flour, then gradually add the soymilk, continuing to stir constantly. Add the salt, then the grated Cashew Cheese, and mix to combine. Cook for 1 minute more, then pour the sauce over the potatoes.

③ **Prepare the breadcrumbs and bake.** Place the toasted whole-grain bread in a food processor, and process until it forms crumbs. Add the olive oil, oregano, thyme, and sea salt, and process several times until well mixed. Sprinkle the breadcrumbs over the top of the casserole and bake uncovered for about 1 hour, or until golden brown and bubbly. (If the breadcrumb topping browns too quickly, cover the casserole with foil.) Serve hot.

Sweet Potato Casserole with Pecan Crumble Topping

Maple syrup, pecans, coconut cream, spices, and coconut oil make this casserole flavorful, celebratory, and memorable.

YIELD: 6-8 SERVINGS

FOR THE SWEET POTATO FILLING:

Two 15-ounce (440 mL) cans coconut milk, refrigerated overnight

1 teaspoon fresh lemon juice

½ teaspoon vanilla extract

5 cups (550 g) cubed sweet potato (approximately 1-inch [2.5 cm] cubes)

Water, for boiling

½ cup (120 mL) pure maple syrup

¼ cup (24 g) finely ground pecans

¾ teaspoon sea salt

1 teaspoon ground cinnamon

¼ teaspoon ground ginger

¼ teaspoon ground nutmeg

2 tablespoons (30 mL) melted coconut oil

FOR THE PECAN CRUMBLE TOPPING:

½ cup (120 mL) coconut oil, at room temperature

¼ cup (50 g) packed brown sugar

¼ cup (60 mL) pure maple syrup

¾ cup (82.5 g) finely chopped pecans

① **Prepare the coconut cream.** Preheat the oven to 325°F (170°C, or gas mark 3). Lightly oil a 9 x 13-inch (23 x 33 cm) casserole dish. Puncture the cans of coconut milk and drain out the liquid. Open the cans and scoop the coconut cream into a small dish. Add the lemon juice and vanilla extract and stir.

② **Make the sweet potatoes.** Place the sweet potatoes in a large pot with water just to cover. Bring the potatoes to a boil, and cook until very tender, 10–15 minutes. Drain the potatoes in a colander, transfer to a food processor, and whip until creamy. Add the maple syrup, finely ground pecans, sea salt, cinnamon, ginger, nutmeg, and coconut oil, processing until smooth and well combined. Add the coconut cream mixture, processing until smooth. Transfer to the prepared casserole dish.

③ **Add the topping.** In a small bowl, combine the coconut oil, brown sugar, maple syrup, and chopped pecans. Spread this topping evenly over the filling and place in the center rack of the oven. Bake for 30–35 minutes, or until the top is golden brown and the casserole is bubbly. Serve hot.

Twice-Baked Cheesy Potatoes

This classic side dish gets a healthy makeover with organic turkey bacon, Cashew Sour Cream, and Cashew Cheese.

YIELD: 8 STUFFED POTATO HALVES

4 large russet potatoes, scrubbed well

8 slices organic turkey bacon

1 cup (230 g) Cashew Sour Cream (page 57) or Coconut Sour Cream (page 57)

½ cup (120 mL) plain unsweetened almond milk or soymilk

½ teaspoon sea salt, plus more to taste

1 cup (260 g) grated Cashew Cheese (page 58)

½ cup (50 g) sliced scallion, white and light green parts only

Freshly ground pepper

1. **Bake the potatoes.** Preheat the oven to 400°F (200°C, or gas mark 6). Wrap the potatoes in aluminum foil and bake for 1 hour 15 minutes, or until baked through completely. Remove from the oven, unwrap the foil, and cool the potatoes before handling. Turn down the oven to 350°F (180°C, or gas mark 4).

2. **Meanwhile, cook the turkey bacon.** Place the turkey bacon in an even layer in a large, heavy-bottomed skillet over medium-high heat, and cook, flipping occasionally, until browned and crispy. Transfer the bacon to a paper towel–lined plate using a slotted spoon or spatula, and crumble or chop the bacon into pieces. Set aside.

3. **Make the filling, then bake again.** Slice the potatoes in half lengthwise, and scoop out the flesh into a large bowl, taking care to keep the skins intact. Place the potato skins on a large baking sheet. Add the Cashew Sour Cream, almond milk, and sea salt to the potato flesh, and mix and mash until creamy. Add the crumbled turkey bacon, grated Cashew Cheese, and sliced scallions, mixing until evenly incorporated. Spoon the filling back into the potato skins on the baking sheet. Sprinkle freshly ground pepper over the top of each potato half, and place in the oven to bake for 15–20 minutes. Serve hot.

Chapter 12

DESSERTS

DAIRY-FREE DESSERTS are often the scariest culinary undertaking for novice dairy-free cooks. Baking demands precision, and changing one ingredient can drastically affect the final outcome. Coconut oil, liquid oils, and margarine each react differently to heat, and a fatty dairy-free milk such as coconut milk yields a different product than a thin dairy-free milk such as rice milk, so many first experiments go awry.

In terms of nutrition, it is almost impossible to consider a dessert health food. Because fat is the backbone of many good desserts, however, making your own desserts makes them at least a bit healthier than those cakes, cookies, and pies that rely on butter, even if they taste just as good. Raw desserts such as raw Avocado Cheesecake (page 163) take healthier desserts to new nutritious heights, and tofu gives Chocolate Peanut Butter Pie (page 151) its creaminess, and coconut oil makes the best Velvety Chocolate Frosting (page 149) ever. Once you dip your spoon into a dish of Coconut Crème Brûlée (page 152) or take your first bite of homemade Mint Chocolate Chip Coconut Milk Ice Cream (page 160), you'll be a believer: the homemade healthier stuff is absolutely delicious, too.

Apple Cobbler Bars

Half pie and half cobber, these bars combine the best of both worlds with a flaky crust and puffed sweet biscuit topping. Plus they're dairy-free and vegan, too.

YIELD: 12–16 BARS

FOR THE COCONUT OIL CRUST:

½ cup (120 mL) coconut oil, warmed

½ cup (112 g) nonhydrogenated soy margarine, room temperature

¾ cup (170 g) light brown sugar

½ teaspoon sea salt

½ teaspoon vanilla extract

2 cups (250 g) all-purpose flour

FOR THE GREEN APPLE FILLING:

5 cups (750 g) chopped peeled green apples

½ teaspoon ground cinnamon

1 tablespoon (15 mL) lemon juice

¾ cup (175 mL) water

½ cup (100 g) unrefined cane sugar

FOR THE OAT TOPPING:

1½ cups (195 g) all-purpose flour

½ cup (40 g) rolled oats

1½ tablespoons (18.4 g) baking powder

¼ cup (50 g) unrefined cane sugar, plus more for sprinkling

6 tablespoons (90 g) coconut oil, at room temperature or slightly warm

½ cup (120 mL) plain unsweetened almond milk or soymilk, at room temperature

① **Make the crust.** Preheat the oven to 325°F (170°C, or gas mark 3). Lightly oil a 9 x 13-inch (23 x 33 cm) casserole dish. Place the coconut oil and the non-hydrogenated soy margarine in a medium bowl. Whip together using an electric hand mixer until creamy. Add the sugar and salt, and stir until smooth. Add the vanilla, mixing until combined. Gradually add the flour until combined. Press into the prepared dish and chill for 30 minutes to set. Bake for 25 minutes, or until lightly golden. Cool the crust completely on a wire cooling rack while preparing the filling and topping. Turn up the oven heat to 350°F (180°C, or gas mark 4).

② **Prepare the apple filling.** Combine all the filling ingredients in a saucepan over medium heat, stirring to dissolve the sugar. Bring to a boil, then turn the heat to low and cook, stirring often, for 8–10 minutes, or until the apples are syrupy and soft but not mushy.

③ **Make the topping.** In a food processor, combine the flour, rolled oats, baking powder, and sugar, pulsing just to mix. Add the coconut oil and process until the mixture is crumbly. With the machine running, add the almond milk until the mixture just holds together and is very soft.

④ **Assemble and bake.** Spread the apple filling evenly over the prepared crust. Using your fingers, pull and flatten pieces of the topping and gently lay them on top of the apple filling. (It is not imperative to cover every inch of the filling, as the topping will expand.) Sprinkle with sugar and bake for 35–40 minutes, or until the cobbler is puffed and golden brown. Cool the bars completely in the pan, then slice into squares and serve.

Chocolate Cupcakes, Three Ways

Peanut Butter, Raspberry, or Velvety Chocolate—take your pick, or make all three! Prepared with a simple yet delectable vegan cupcake base, these will yield delicious dairy-free cupcakes that will satisfy any chocolate cupcake craving no matter which variation you choose.

YIELD: 12 CUPCAKES

FOR THE CHOCOLATE CUPCAKES:

1 cup (125 g) all-purpose flour

⅓ cup (42 g) unsweetened cocoa powder

¾ teaspoon baking soda

½ teaspoon baking powder

¼ teaspoon sea salt

1 cup (235 mL) coconut milk

½ cup (100 g) unrefined cane sugar

¼ cup (60 mL) maple syrup, at room temperature

⅓ cup (80 mL) coconut oil, melted

1 teaspoon cider vinegar

1 teaspoon pure vanilla extract

FOR THE PEANUT BUTTER FROSTING:

⅓ cup (80 g) creamy peanut butter, at room temperature

⅓ cup (80 mL) coconut oil, melted

2½–3 cups (300–360 g) confectioners' sugar

2–3 tablespoons (30–45 mL) unsweetened almond milk, at room temperature

FOR THE RASPBERRY FROSTING:

½ cup (112 g) nonhydrogenated soy margarine

¼ cup (32 g) fresh raspberries

2–3 cups (240–360 g) confectioners' sugar

1 tablespoon (15 mL) unsweetened almond milk, or as needed

FOR THE VELVETY CHOCOLATE FROSTING:

2 cups (240 g) confectioners' sugar

¾ cup unsweetened (90 g) cocoa powder

¼ cup (60 mL) coconut oil, melted

¼ cup (60 mL) unsweetened almond milk, at room temperature

½ teaspoon vanilla

① **Make the chocolate cupcakes.** Preheat the oven to 350°F (180°C, or gas mark 4). Line a 12-cup muffin tray with cupcake liners. In a large bowl, sift together the flour, cocoa powder, baking soda, baking powder, and sea salt. In another bowl, whisk together the coconut milk, unrefined cane sugar, maple syrup, melted coconut oil, cider vinegar, and vanilla extract. Add the dry ingredients to the wet, mixing until just combined. Use a portion scoop to fill the cupcake liners, filling each about three-quarters of the way full. Bake for 15–20 minutes, or until the cakes spring back slightly when touched. Cool the cupcakes completely on a wire cooling rack before topping with the desired frosting.

2. **To make the Peanut Butter Frosting:** Place the peanut butter and melted coconut oil in a large bowl. Using an electric hand mixer, beat them together. Add the confectioners' sugar gradually and then the almond milk, until the frosting becomes smooth and creamy. Use immediately.

To make the Raspberry Frosting: Place the soy margarine in a large bowl and beat until creamy. Add the raspberries, confectioners' sugar, and almond milk, beating well until the frosting comes together and is thick and creamy. Refrigerate the frosting for 10 minutes before using.

To make the Velvety Chocolate Frosting: Mix together the confectioners' sugar and cocoa powder in a large bowl. Add the coconut oil, and beat until the mixture comes together but is stiff and clumpy. Add the almond milk and vanilla, and beat until a smooth, creamy mixture is formed. Use immediately.

Chocolate Coconut Milk Pudding

This rich, decadent pudding is simple enough for weekday desserts but also easy to dress up for dinner parties. Toasted coconut flakes take just minutes to prepare and add an extra touch of glamor.

YIELD: 4 SERVINGS

FOR THE TOASTED COCONUT FLAKES:

1 cup (80 g) large coconut flakes

FOR THE CHOCOLATE COCONUT MILK PUDDING:

3 tablespoons (24 g) cornstarch

3 tablespoons (45 mL) cold water

One 15-ounce (440 mL) can light coconut milk

⅓ cup (67 mL) and 2 tablespoons (26 g) organic sugar

¼ cup (50 g) unsweetened cocoa powder

Pinch of salt

½ cup (120 mL) plain unsweetened almond milk

⅓ cup (58 g) dairy-free chocolate chips

½ teaspoon coconut extract

Dairy-free dark chocolate shavings, for garnish

1. **Prepare the toasted coconut.** Preheat the oven to 350°F (180°C, or gas mark 4). Spread the coconut flakes on an ungreased cookie sheet and bake for 3–5 minutes, or until lightly browned. Remove and cool the flakes completely. (If making in advance, store flakes in an airtight container at room temperature for up to 3 days.)

2. **Make the pudding.** In a small bowl, whisk together the cornstarch and water until dissolved. In a small saucepan over medium heat, combine the coconut milk, sugar, cocoa powder, and salt. Stirring constantly, gradually add the almond milk until the pudding is smooth. Cook, continuing to stir, until steam begins to rise from the surface of the pudding and a thin film forms. Remove from the heat before the pudding comes to a boil. Add the chocolate chips, swirling a few times to keep the chips from resting on the bottom of the pan, but do not stir. Rest for 3 minutes, then stir to incorporate the melted chocolate. Stir in the cornstarch mixture and coconut extract, and return the pan to medium heat. Stirring constantly, cook for just 2–3 minutes longer, or until the pudding thickens.

3. **Cool.** Transfer the pudding to a heat-proof dish and cover with plastic wrap (press the plastic wrap directly on the surface of the pudding to prevent a skin from forming). Cool the pudding for 15–20 minutes at room temperature, then chill for 2–3 hours, or until set. Serve the pudding cold with toasted coconut and dairy-free dark chocolate shavings.

Chocolate Peanut Butter Pie

Every vegan and dairy-free enthusiast has a version of the classic peanut butter tofu pie. This is mine, prepared with a coconut oil graham cracker crust, simple chocolate ganache layer, and creamy peanut butter filling. It's topped with a pretty swirl of chocolate, so be sure to set about a quarter of the chocolate filling aside.

YIELD: ONE 9-INCH (23 CM) PIE, 8 SERVINGS

FOR THE GRAHAM CRACKER CRUST:

1½ cups (180 g) dairy-free graham cracker crumbs

⅓ cup (75 g) unrefined cane sugar

½ cup (120 mL) coconut oil, melted

FOR THE CHOCOLATE LAYER:

1 cup (235 mL) unsweetened hemp milk, soymilk, or full-fat coconut milk

2½ cups (525 g) dairy-free dark chocolate chips

¼ cup (60 mL) maple syrup

FOR THE PEANUT BUTTER LAYER:

One 15-ounce (440 mL) can full-fat coconut milk, refrigerated overnight

One 12.3-ounce (349 g) box firm silken tofu

1⅓ cups (320 g) creamy peanut butter

¼ cup (50 g) organic unrefined cane sugar

⅓ cup (40 g) confectioners' sugar

Dairy-free dark chocolate shavings, for garnish

① **Make the graham cracker crust.** Preheat the oven to 350°F (180°C, or gas mark 4). Lightly grease a 9-inch (23 cm) pie plate. In a small bowl, combine the graham cracker crumbs, sugar, and melted coconut oil, mixing with your fingers until it just starts to hold together. Press the crust into the prepared pie plate and bake for 8–10 minutes, or until lightly browned. Cool completely.

② **Prepare the chocolate layer.** Place the dairy-free milk, chocolate chips, and maple syrup in a small saucepan over low heat. Cook, stirring constantly, until the chocolate melts completely and looks glossy. Remove the pan from the heat, transfer the chocolate filling to a heat-proof bowl, and cool at room temperature, stirring occasionally, for 30 minutes. Pour half the filling into the bottom of the prepared crust, brushing the filling gently up the sides to completely cover. Place the crust in the refrigerator for 30 minutes. Brush half the remaining filling on top of the first layer of chocolate. (The chocolate filling will still be a bit runny at this point, so if you pour it all in at once, it will pool on the bottom.) Return the pie to the refrigerator for 30 minutes. You should have a quarter of the total filling left, which you'll use later as a topping.

③ **Make the peanut butter layer.** Puncture the can of coconut milk and drain out the liquid. Scoop out ½ cup (120 mL) of the coconut cream into a small bowl. Place the silken tofu in a blender and process until smooth. Add the peanut butter, sugars, and coconut cream, and blend until very smooth and creamy. Pour on top of the chocolate filling. Drizzle the remaining chocolate filing on top, swirling some of it gently with a spatula to create a pattern. Chill for 2 hours, or until set. Top with chocolate shavings and serve cold.

Coconut Crème Brûlée

Coconut cream and egg yolks make this custard a rich affair of flavor and creamy texture. For dinner parties, prepare, bake, and chill the custards the night before and then just pop them under the broiler and back into the fridge a couple of hours before you're ready to serve.

YIELD: 4 SERVINGS

6 egg yolks

½ cup (100 g) granulated sugar, divided

½ teaspoon vanilla extract

Three 15-ounce (440 mL) cans full-fat coconut milk, refrigerated overnight

① **Prepare the dishes.** Preheat the oven to 300°F (150°C, or gas mark 2). Set 4 crème brûlée dishes on a rimmed baking sheet or in a large casserole dish. Fill the bottom part of a double boiler with water and bring to a simmer.

② **Make the custard.** In a small bowl, beat the egg yolks with ¼ cup (50 g) of the sugar and vanilla until thick and pale yellow in color. Puncture the cans of coconut milk and drain out the liquid. Open the cans and scoop out the coconut cream (you should have about 2½ cups [590 g]) into a small saucepan and heat over low heat until it almost comes to a boil but does not boil. Remove the pan from the heat. Stir half of the coconut cream into the egg yolk mixture, whisking vigorously to avoid cooking the eggs. Pour in the remaining coconut cream, whisking to combine. Transfer the custard in to the top of the double boiler and heat over the simmering water, stirring constantly, for 2–3 minutes, or until the custard is slightly thinner than pudding, but coats the back of a spoon. (If your custard becomes bubbly or frothy, it's been overwhisked; let it sit on the counter for a few minutes to settle down, and then continue.)

③ **Bake the custards.** Pour the custard into the prepared crème brûlée dishes, place the baking sheet into the oven, and bake for 30 minutes. Cool the custards completely, then refrigerate overnight.

④ **Broil the tops.** Preheat the broiler. Sprinkle the custards with the remaining ¼ cup (50 g) sugar. Place the dishes under the broiler until the sugar melts, 2–3 minutes, taking care not to let the sugar burn (it's okay to have spots of burnt sugar on the top, you just don't want to have a completely blackened crème brûlée). Cool the custards, and then refrigerate for 1–2 hours, or until set. Serve cold.

Cream-Filled Chocolate Cupcakes

This vegan version of the packaged cream-filled favorite is a fun treat and slightly healthier to boot. For the best results, serve these cupcakes within a day or two.

YIELD: 12 CUPCAKES

FOR THE CREAM FILLING:

Two 15-ounce (440 mL) cans coconut milk

1 cup (235 mL) unsweetened almond milk, divided

⅓ cup (67 g) unrefined cane sugar

⅛ teaspoon sea salt

1 teaspoon vanilla extract

3 tablespoons (24 g) cornstarch

FOR THE CHOCOLATE CUPCAKES:

1 cup (125 g) all-purpose flour

⅓ cup (42 g) cocoa powder

¾ teaspoon baking soda

½ teaspoon baking powder

¼ teaspoon sea salt

1 cup (235 mL) coconut milk

½ cup (100 g) unrefined cane sugar

¼ cup (50 g) organic brown sugar

⅓ cup (80 mL) canola oil

1 teaspoon each cider vinegar and pure vanilla extract

FOR THE CHOCOLATE TOPPING:

1 cup (235 mL) unsweetened hemp milk or soymilk, or full-fat coconut milk

2½ cups (438 g) dairy-free dark chocolate chips

① **Prepare the cream filling.** Puncture the cans of coconut milk and drain out the liquid. Scoop out the coconut cream and place in a small saucepan with ¾ cup (175 mL) of the almond milk and the sugar, salt, and vanilla. In a small bowl, mix together the remaining almond milk and the cornstarch until dissolved, and pour into the saucepan. Place the saucepan over medium heat and cook, stirring constantly, until thickened, about 5 minutes. Pour into the dish and place plastic wrap directly on the surface. Chill until set, 3–4 hours.

② **Make the cupcakes.** Preheat the oven to 350°F (180°C, or gas mark 4). Line a muffin tin with cupcake liners. In a bowl, sift together the dry ingredients. In another bowl, mix together the coconut milk, sugars, oil, vinegar, and vanilla. Mix the dry ingredients with the wet until smooth. Pour into cupcake liners until three-quarters full. Bake for 15–20 minutes, or until the cupcakes spring back slightly when touched. Cool completely.

③ **Make the chocolate topping.** Place the milk and chocolate chips in a saucepan over low heat. Cook, stirring constantly, until the chocolate has completely melted and looks glossy. Transfer to a heat-proof bowl and chill, stirring occasionally, for 30 minutes.

④ **Assemble the cupcakes.** Using a sharp knife, make a 1-inch (2.5 cm) circle in the top of a cupcake, angling downward so that it comes to a point. Remove this piece and repeat with remaining cupcakes. Spoon 2 tablespoons (30 g) of the cream filling into each cupcake, then replace the tops. Chill for 10 minutes. Spread the chocolate topping over the cupcakes, then return to the refrigerator for 15 minutes longer to chill. Serve cold.

Extra-Nutty Carrot Cake
with Cashew Cream Cheese Icing

Spiced with warming cinnamon and ginger, bedecked with walnuts, coconut, and pecans, and prepared with healthy ingredients such as dates, carrots, and coconut oil, this carrot cake is one of the healthiest and most flavorful you'll ever eat.

YIELD: ONE 9-INCH (23 CM) CAKE, 10-12 SERVINGS

FOR THE CAKE:

1 tablespoon (59 mL) coconut oil or margarine

1 cup (178 g) chopped pitted Medjool dates

Boiling water, for soaking

¾ cup (180 mL) maple syrup

½ cup (120 mL) coconut oil, melted

1 teaspoon vanilla extract

1 teaspoon lemon juice

3 large eggs

1¼ cups (156 g) all-purpose flour

½ cup (62 g) whole-wheat pastry flour

1 teaspoon ground cinnamon

½ teaspoon ground ginger

¾ teaspoon baking powder

¾ teaspoon sea salt

1 cup (95 g) ground walnuts

1 cup (80 g) shredded coconut

½ cup (55 g) finely chopped pecans

1 heaping cup (110 g) grated carrot

½ cup (72 g) golden raisins

FOR THE CASHEW CREAM CHEESE ICING:

½ cup (115 g) Cashew Cream Cheese (page 63)

½ cup (112 g) nonhydrogenated margarine, softened

3½ cups (420 g) confectioners' sugar

¼ cup (60 mL) unsweetened almond milk

½ teaspoon vanilla extract

1 **Make the cake.** Preheat the oven to 325°F (170°C, or gas mark 3). Lightly grease a 10-inch (25 cm) springform pan with the coconut oil. Place the chopped dates in a small bowl and pour boiling water over the top just to cover. Let soak for 15-20 minutes. Blend the dates and soaking liquid with the maple syrup, melted coconut oil, vanilla extract, and lemon juice until smooth. Add the eggs, one at a time, beating until smooth.

2 **Add the wet ingredients to the dry ingredients.** In a large bowl, combine the flours, cinnamon, ginger, baking powder, and sea salt. Add the ground walnuts, shredded coconut, and chopped pecans. Pour in the liquid ingredients and stir to mix well. Fold in the grated carrot and raisins.

3 **Bake.** Pour into the prepared springform pan and bake until the top of the cake springs back when touched, about 30-40 minutes. Cool the cake completely before frosting.

4 **Make the icing.** Place the Cashew Cream Cheese and nonhydrogenated margarine in a large bowl. Using an electric hand mixer, beat together until combined. Gradually add the confectioners' sugar and beat for about 3 minutes, or until the icing starts to come together and gets a little clumpy. Add the almond milk and vanilla extract and beat until smooth. Spread over the cooled cake with an offset spatula.

Gingerbread with Vanilla Glaze

Blackstrap molasses is a rich source of calcium and gives this dairy-free cake a flavorful bite. Serve with a generous dose of vanilla glaze drizzled over top, or for a humbler cake, just top with a sprinkling of confectioners' sugar.

YIELD: ONE 9-INCH (23 CM) SQUARE CAKE, 10–12 SERVINGS

FOR THE GINGERBREAD:

2½ cups (312 g) all-purpose flour

1½ teaspoons baking soda

1 teaspoon ground cinnamon

1 teaspoon ground ginger

½ teaspoon ground cloves

½ teaspoon sea salt

½ cup (112 g) nonhydrogenated soy margarine

½ cup (100 g) granulated sugar

2 large organic eggs, lightly beaten

1 cup (340 g) blackstrap molasses

1 cup (235 mL) coconut milk

FOR THE VANILLA GLAZE:

1½ cups (180 g) confectioners' sugar

2½ tablespoons (38 mL) unsweetened almond milk or soymilk

½ teaspoon vanilla extract

① **Make the gingerbread.** Preheat the oven to 350°F (180°C, or gas mark 4). Lightly grease and flour a 9-inch (23 cm) square cake pan. Set aside. In a medium bowl, sift the flour, baking soda, cinnamon, ginger, cloves, and sea salt, and mix well. In the bowl of a stand mixer, beat together the margarine and granulated sugar until fluffy. Add the eggs and beat well, followed by the molasses and coconut milk. Add the dry ingredients to the wet ingredients, mixing until just combined. Pour into the prepared cake pan and bake for 1 hour, or until a toothpick inserted into the center of the cake comes out clean. Cool the gingerbread for 20 minutes before icing.

② **Make the icing.** In a medium bowl, beat together the confectioners' sugar with the almond milk and vanilla extract until smooth. Pour over the finished gingerbread and let the icing set for about 15 minutes. Cut into 10–12 slices and serve.

Hometown Yellow Cupcakes with Vanilla Frosting

I call these "hometown" cupcakes because they remind me of the traditional yellow cupcakes that appear on tables year-round all across the United States. Although these don't contain tons of butter like the classic, they still taste good.

YIELD: 24 CUPCAKES

FOR THE CUPCAKES:

3 cups (375 g) all-purpose flour

1 tablespoon (18 g) baking powder

1 teaspoon sea salt

½ cup (120 mL) coconut oil

1½ cups (300 g) unrefined cane sugar

4 large eggs

⅓ cup (80 mL) canola oil

1 teaspoon vanilla extract

½ cup (120 mL) plain almond milk

FOR THE VANILLA FROSTING:

¾ cup (178 mL) coconut oil, warmed

6 cups (720 g) confectioners' sugar

1 teaspoon vanilla extract

¼–½ cup (60–120 mL) almond milk, as needed

① **Prepare the trays.** Preheat the oven to 350°F (180°C, or gas mark 4). Line 2 standard 12-cup muffin trays with cupcake liners.

② **Make the cupcakes.** Place the flour, baking powder, and sea salt in a bowl, and stir just to combine. In the bowl of a stand mixer, beat the coconut oil and sugar until smooth. Add the eggs, one at a time, beating well with each addition. Add the canola oil and vanilla and mix well. Turn the mixer speed to low. Add half the dry ingredients, mixing just until combined, then add the almond milk, followed by the remaining dry ingredients. Mix just until the batter comes together. Use a portion scoop to fill the cupcake liners, filling each about three-quarters full. Bake until the tops of the cupcakes spring back slightly when touched, 20–25 minutes. Cool the cupcakes completely on a wire cooling rack before frosting.

③ **Make the frosting.** In a large bowl or the bowl of a stand mixer, beat the coconut oil with the confectioners' sugar, vanilla extract, and ¼ cup (60 mL) of almond milk. Beat until the icing comes together, adding ¼ cup (60 mL) more almond milk, 1 tablespoon (15 mL) at a time, if needed. Chill for 10 minutes, then frost the cupcakes. Serve the cupcakes cold or at room temperature.

Homemade Dairy-Free Ice Cream, Three Ways

Making your own ice cream with an ice cream maker is easy; once you've done it, you'll never want to buy store-bought again. These three variations are healthier versions of three traditional ice cream flavors, but the variations are endless. Use the base recipe and experiment with different flavors and additions.

YIELD: 1 QUART (0.9 L), 8 SERVINGS

FOR THE ICE CREAM BASE:

Two 15-ounce (440 mL) cans full-fat coconut milk

1 cup (235 mL) unsweetened almond milk

1 cup (200 g) granulated sugar

½ teaspoon salt

FOR CHOCOLATE ICE CREAM:

½ cup (60 g) unsweetened cocoa powder

½ cup (50 g) shaved good-quality dairy-free dark chocolate

FOR STRAWBERRY ICE CREAM:

2 cups (340 g) mashed fresh strawberries, divided

FOR VANILLA BEAN ICE CREAM:

1 vanilla bean

① **Make the ice cream base.** In the bowl of standing mixer or a large bowl using an electric hand mixer, combine the coconut milk, almond milk, sugar, and salt.

② **Chose your flavor and incorporate.** For the Chocolate Ice Cream, add the unsweetened cocoa powder. For the Strawberry Ice Cream, add 1 cup (170 g) of the mashed strawberries. Mix until the sugar has dissolved, about 3 minutes. Place the bowl in the refrigerator for 30 minutes. For the Vanilla Bean Ice Cream, add the vanilla bean and place the cream base in a saucepan over medium heat. Use a candy thermometer and heat until it reads 175°F (79°C), stirring often to dissolve the sugar. Carefully remove the hull from the vanilla bean. Transfer the base to a heat-proof dish, cover, and refrigerate overnight.

③ **Place in an ice cream maker, and freeze.** Pour the flavored base of your choice into the bowl of an ice cream maker and follow the manufacturer's instructions. For the Chocolate Ice Cream, in the last 5 minutes of churning, add the shaved chocolate or stop the machine and fold in by hand. For the Strawberry Ice Cream, in the last 5 minutes of churning, add the remaining 1 cup (170 g) strawberries or fold them in by hand. Transfer the ice cream to a covered glass storage dish and freeze for 1–2 hours, or until ready to serve.

Mint Chocolate Chip Coconut Milk Ice Cream

Mint is one of those flavors that you see a lot in winter, but I consider this ice cream one of my favorites to prepare year-round, for both summer festivities as well as winter occasions. I love having an ice cream maker at my disposal as a dairy-free home cook. With hardly any effort or time, I can have a delicious, healthier variation of a favorite indulgence.

YIELD: 1 QUART (0.9 L), 8 SERVINGS

2 cups (475 mL) full-fat coconut milk

2 cups (475 mL) unsweetened almond milk

1 cup (200 g) granulated sugar

½ teaspoon salt

½ teaspoon peppermint extract

1 cup (175 g) mini dairy-free chocolate chips

Fresh mint leaves, for garnishing (optional)

① **Make the base.** In the bowl of stand mixer, combine the coconut milk, almond milk, sugar, salt, and peppermint extract. Mix until the sugar has dissolved, about 3 minutes. Place the bowl in the refrigerator for 30 minutes.

② **Place in an ice cream maker, and freeze.** Pour the ice cream base into the bowl of an ice cream maker and follow the manufacturer's instructions. In the last 5 minutes of churning, add the mini chocolate chips or stop the machine and fold them in by hand. Transfer the ice cream to a covered glass storage dish and freeze for 1–2 hours, or until ready to serve. Garnish with fresh mint leaves, if desired.

Mexican Chocolate Cake with Avocado Frosting

Avocado frosting adds fun color and flavor to this moist, spicy vegan chocolate cake—and cuts out the butter of traditional frostings. Top your creation with dark chocolate shavings, coconut shavings, chocolate-dipped strawberries, or Cinnamon-Sugar Stars (page 172) for extra festive flair.

YIELD: 1 DOUBLE-LAYER 8-INCH (20 CM) CAKE, 10-12 SERVINGS

FOR THE MEXICAN CHOCOLATE CAKE:

1½ cups (355 mL) almond milk or soymilk

2 tablespoons (30 mL) cider vinegar

3 cups (375 g) all-purpose flour

2 cups (400 g) granulated sugar

1 cup (128 g) unsweetened cocoa powder, plus extra for pan

1 tablespoon (7 g) ground cinnamon

2 teaspoons baking soda

¼ teaspoon cayenne pepper

½ teaspoon salt

1 cup (235 mL) coffee at room temperature

½ cup (120 mL) canola oil or extra-virgin olive oil

1 tablespoon (15 mL) vanilla extract

FOR THE AVOCADO FROSTING:

1 cup (225 g) nonhydrogenated dairy-free margarine

7 cups (840 g) confectioners' sugar, sifted

⅔ cup (97 g) well-mashed fresh avocado

2 teaspoons (10 mL) lemon juice

1 **Prepare the chocolate cake.** Preheat the oven to 350°F (180°C, or gas mark 4). Lightly grease two 8-inch (20 cm) round springform cake pans and sprinkle with cocoa powder, tapping out the excess. In a small bowl, combine the dairy-free milk with the cider vinegar. In a large bowl, combine the flour, sugar, cocoa powder, ground cinnamon, baking soda, cayenne pepper, and salt. Add the coffee, canola oil, vanilla extract, and milk mixture to the dry ingredients and stir until smooth. Portion the batter equally into the prepared cake pans and bake until the tops of the cakes spring back when touched, about 25–30 minutes. Cool the cakes for 20–30 minutes in the pans, then carefully remove the cakes and cool them completely on a wire cooling rack.

2 **Prepare the avocado frosting.** Beat the dairy-free margarine in the bowl of a stand mixer until fluffy and smooth. Gradually add half the confectioners' sugar, followed by the mashed avocado, lemon juice, and the remaining half of the confectioners' sugar, beating until smooth and creamy. Cover and chill immediately until ready to use. (Avocado frosting should be used on the same day it is made.)

3 **Frost the cakes.** Prepare the avocado frosting. Frost the top of one of the cake layers with avocado frosting. Place the other cake top side up on top of the frosted cake, then frost the sides and top. Serve cold or at room temperature.

Lemon Meringue Pie

Lemon meringue is such a beautiful, impressive pie that never disappoints, and this one, with hints of coconut in the filling and crust, takes the tart and sweet flavors to new heights.

YIELD: ONE 9-INCH (23 CM) PIE, 8 SERVINGS

FOR THE GRAHAM CRACKER CRUST:

1½ cups (180 g) dairy-free graham cracker crumbs

⅓ cup (60 g) unrefined cane sugar

½ cup (120 mL) coconut oil, melted

FOR THE LEMON FILLING:

2 cups (400 g) unrefined cane sugar

¼ cup (32 g) flour

6 tablespoons (48 g) cornstarch

½ teaspoon salt

1 cup (235 mL) water

2 cups (475 mL) lemon juice

¼ cup (60 mL) coconut oil

8 large egg yolks

FOR THE MERINGUE:

8 large egg whites

Pinch of cream of tartar

½ cup (100 g) sugar

① **Make the graham cracker crust.** Preheat the oven to 350°F (180°C, or gas mark 4). Lightly grease a 9-inch (23 cm) pie plate with coconut oil. In a small bowl, combine the graham cracker crumbs, sugar, and melted coconut oil, mixing with your fingers until it just starts to hold together. Press the crust into the prepared pie plate and bake for 8–10 minutes, or until lightly browned.

② **Make the lemon filling.** In a medium saucepan over medium heat, combine the sugar, flour, cornstarch, and salt until well mixed. Whisk in the water and lemon juice. Cook, stirring constantly, until the sugar is dissolved and the liquid nearly comes to a boil but does not boil. Add the coconut oil and stir just until melted. Remove the pan from the heat. In a medium bowl, whisk the egg yolks. Gradually whisk in one-third of the hot lemon mixture, whisking constantly to avoid cooking the eggs. Whisk in the rest of the lemon mixture, then return to the saucepan over medium heat. Whisking constantly, bring the filling to a low boil and cook until thickened. Pour the filling into the prepared crust.

③ **Make the meringue.** In the bowl of a stand mixer, beat the egg whites with the cream of tartar on medium speed until foamy. Gradually add the sugar, and beat until stiff peaks form, 8–10 minutes. Using a spatula, add dollops of the meringue on top of the filling until the pie is totally covered with marvelous meringue peaks. Bake for 7–10 minutes, or until golden brown. Refrigerate the pie for 2 hours before serving. Serve cold.

Raw Avocado Cheesecake with Date Nut Crust

This cheesecake is one of the most expensive I ever make (and certainly the healthiest), so I save it for special occasions. It's not overly sweet, so if you want a sweeter cake, add a sweetener such as Stevia or maple syrup until it tastes right to you. Feel free to pour in a cup of raspberries or strawberries and puree with the rest of the filling to make other varieties.

YIELD: ONE 9-INCH (23 CM) CAKE, 10–12 SERVINGS

FOR THE DATE NUT CRUST:

Shredded unsweetened coconut

1 cup (135 g) macadamia nuts

1 cup (135 g) walnuts

1 cup (178 g) finely chopped dates

¼ teaspoon sea salt

2 tablespoons (30 g) raw tahini

FOR THE AVOCADO CHEESECAKE FILLING:

1 cup (95 g) finely ground cashews

¾ cup (180 mL) coconut oil, warm (not heated above 90°F [32°C])

8 large ripe avocados, peeled, pitted, and mashed well

½ cup (120 mL) orange juice

¼ cup (60 mL) fresh lime juice

1 cup (235 g) agave or maple syrup, or to taste

Pinch of sea salt

1 **Prepare the date nut crust.** Lightly grease a 9-inch (23 cm) springform pan with coconut oil. Sprinkle the pan generously with unsweetened coconut. Place the macadamia nuts and walnuts in a blender, and blend until crumbly. Add the dates, sea salt, and tahini, and blend until the mixture sticks together in a chunky paste. Press the crust into the pan.

2 **Prepare the avocado cheesecake filling.** Place the finely ground cashews, coconut oil, avocados, orange juice, lime juice, syrup, and sea salt in a blender or food processor, and process until very creamy. Pour into the prepared crust and place in the refrigerator for 2 hours, or until set. Serve cold.

Beet Red Velvet Cupcakes with Soy Cream Cheese Frosting

These cupcakes are less red than ones that call for an entire bottle of red food dye, but the naturally bright red color of beets lends a nice crimson hue.

YIELD: 24 CUPCAKES

FOR THE BEET RED VELVET CUPCAKES:

3 medium beets, scrubbed and leaves removed

2 cups (250 g) all-purpose flour

½ cup (64 g) unsweetened cocoa powder

1 teaspoon baking soda

½ teaspoon salt

4 large eggs

1 cup (200 g) organic unrefined cane sugar

1 cup (235 g) maple syrup, at room temperature

1 cup (230 g) soy yogurt or coconut yogurt, at room temperature

½ cup (120 mL) coconut milk

1 tablespoon (15 mL) lemon juice

1 cup (236 mL) coconut oil, melted

FOR THE SOY CREAM CHEESE FROSTING:

One 8-ounce (225 g) container dairy-free soy cream cheese

½ cup (112 g) nonhydrogenated soy margarine

3½ cups (420 g) confectioners' sugar

1 teaspoon vanilla extract

① **Roast the beets.** Preheat the oven to 400°F (200°C, or gas mark 6). Place the beets in a small baking dish and add about 1 inch (2.5 cm) of water. Cover with foil and bake for 1 hour, or until the beets are tender and can be pierced with a knife. Once the beets are cool enough to handle, cut them into large chunks and place into a blender or food processor with 3–4 tablespoons (45–60 mL) of the beet water. Puree until smooth.

② **Make the cupcakes.** Turn down the heat to 350°F (180°C, or gas mark 4). Line 2 standard 12-cup muffin tins with cupcakes liners. In a large bowl, sift together the flour, cocoa powder, baking soda, and salt. In another bowl, whisk the eggs very well. Add the sugar to the eggs, and beat for 3–4 minutes, or until pale yellow and well combined. Add the maple syrup, soy yogurt, coconut milk, lemon juice, and melted coconut oil, and beat well. Add the wet ingredients and the beet puree to the dry ingredients, stirring just to combine.

③ **Bake.** Using a measuring cup, portion the batter into the prepared tins. Bake for 18–20 minutes, or until the cupcakes spring back when touched. Cool the cupcakes completely on a wire cooling rack before frosting.

④ **Make the frosting.** In the bowl of a stand mixer, beat the soy cream cheese with the soy margarine until smooth. Gradually add the confectioners' sugar, beating well with each addition, and then add the vanilla extract and beat on high until the mixture is thick and creamy, adding more confectioners sugar if necessary. Chill the icing for 10 minutes before using to frost the cupcakes. Serve cold or at room temperature.

Pecan-Crusted Ice Cream Cake

Whether you use store-bought dairy-free ice cream or homemade for this cake, no one will guess that it's dairy free. Layers of ice cream and rich chocolate filling, all on top of a graham–pecan crust, make this cake a celebration in itself.

YIELD: ONE 9-INCH (12 CM) CAKE, 12 SERVINGS

FOR THE GRAHAM-PECAN CRUST:

1½ cups (180 g) dairy-free graham cracker crumbs

1 cup (110 g) finely chopped pecans

¼ cup (50 g) unrefined cane sugar

½ cup (120 mL) coconut oil, melted

FOR THE CHOCOLATE FILLING:

Two 15-ounce (440 mL) cans coconut milk, refrigerated overnight

¼ cup (60 mL) maple syrup

10 ounces (283 g) dairy-free dark chocolate, finely chopped

FOR THE ICE CREAM LAYERS:

4 cups (560 g) Vanilla Bean Ice Cream (page 158), softened, divided

4 cups (560 g) Chocolate Ice Cream (page 158), softened, divided

① **Prepare the crust.** Preheat the oven to 350°F (180°C, or gas mark 4). Lightly grease the bottom and sides of a 9-inch (23 cm) springform pan with coconut oil. Combine the graham cracker crumbs, pecans, and sugar in a food processor or blender, and pulse until the pecans are ground and the ingredients are well mixed. Add the melted coconut oil, and pulse until the crust comes together in moist crumbs. Press evenly into the bottom of the prepared springform pan and up the sides. Bake for 10 minutes, or until the crust is golden brown. Cool the crust completely.

② **Prepare the chocolate filling.** Puncture the cans of coconut milk and drain out the liquid. Place 1 cup (235 mL) coconut cream and the maple syrup in a small saucepan over medium heat, and stir to combine. Heat until steam rises from the surface but it does not boil. Place the dark chocolate in a heat-proof bowl, and pour the coconut cream over the top. Let rest undisturbed for 5 minutes. Stir the filling until it is completely smooth, and cool at room temperature for 45 minutes, stirring every 15 minutes.

③ **Assemble.** Spread 3 cups (420 g) of the Vanilla Bean Ice Cream on top of the cooled crust. Spoon about ¾ cup (180 mL) of the chocolate filling over the top. Place the cake in the freezer for 10–15 minutes, or until the chocolate filling has set. (Keep remaining ice cream in the refrigerator or refreeze if necessary to keep it from melting.) Spread 3 cups (420 g) of the Chocolate Ice Cream on top of the filling, followed by another ¾ cup (180 mL) chocolate filling. Return the cake to the freezer for 10–15 minutes, or until the chocolate filling has set. Top with the remaining Chocolate Ice Cream and remaining 1 cup (140 g) Vanilla Bean Ice Cream, swirling the two to combine slightly. Top with the remaining chocolate filling, smoothing with a spoon or offset spatula. Freeze overnight. Let the cake sit at room temperature for 5–10 minutes before cutting.

Super-Thick Milkshakes Three Ways

Flavored with chocolate, peanut butter and chocolate, or just vanilla, super-thick no-moo shakes are treats that people of all ages enjoy. Top with a flourish of Coconut Milk Whipped Cream.

YIELD: FOUR MILKSHAKES, 4 SERVINGS

FOR THE CHOCOLATE MILKSHAKE:

4 cups (560 g) Chocolate Ice Cream (page 158) or store-bought dairy-free chocolate coconut milk ice cream

¼ cup (60 mL) coconut cream

½ teaspoon vanilla extract

FOR THE PEANUT BUTTER
CHOCOLATE MILKSHAKE:

2 cups (280 g) Chocolate Ice Cream (page 158) or store-bought dairy-free chocolate ice cream

2 cups (280 g) Vanilla Bean Ice Cream (page 158) or store-bought dairy-free vanilla coconut milk ice cream

¼ cup (60 g) creamy peanut butter

¼ cup (60 mL) coconut cream

¼ teaspoon vanilla extract

FOR THE VANILLA MILKSHAKE:

4 cups (560 g) Vanilla Bean Ice Cream (page 158) or store-bought dairy-free vanilla coconut milk ice cream

¼ cup (60 mL) coconut cream

½ teaspoon vanilla extract

Coconut Milk Whipped Cream, optional (recipe follows)

① **Make the milkshake.** Choose your flavor and place all ingredients in a blender. Process until creamy and smooth. Serve immediately with Coconut Milk Whipped Cream, if desired.

COCONUT MILK WHIPPED CREAM

Creamy, simple, and healthy, Coconut Milk Whipped Cream is one of the easiest way to add a little bit of flair to your dairy-free desserts. Plan in advance, as the cream and bowl are chilled overnight.

YIELD: 2 CUPS (160 G) WHIPPED CREAM

Two cans full-fat coconut milk, refrigerated overnight

1 tablespoon (8 g) confectioners' sugar

Mixing bowl, refrigerated overnight

Scoop out the coconut cream from the coconut milk cans into the refrigerated mixing bowl. Discard the liquid. Sprinkle the confectioners' sugar into the bowl. Beat on high until peaks form, and serve immediately.

Vegan Cheesecake with Graham Cracker Crust

This is one of those recipes that's so easy to make that it feels like cheating. But, it's really good. If you are not vegan, feel free to use three real eggs instead of the egg replacer.

YIELD: ONE 9-INCH (23 CM) CAKE, 10-12 SERVINGS

FOR THE GRAHAM CRACKER CRUST:

1½ cups (180 g) dairy-free graham cracker crumbs

⅓ cup (67 g) unrefined cane sugar

½ cup (120 mL) coconut oil, melted

FOR THE CHEESECAKE FILLING:

32 ounces (0.9 kg) store-bought soy cream cheese

1¼ cups (250 g) granulated sugar

Egg substitute for 4 eggs

⅓ cup (77 g) store-bought soy sour cream, plus more for spreading

1 teaspoon vanilla extract

① **Make the crust.** Preheat the oven to 350°F (180°C, or gas mark 4). Grease a 9-inch (23 cm) springform pan with coconut oil. In a medium bowl, mix together the graham cracker crumbs and cane sugar. Add the melted coconut oil, and stir until the mixture just holds together slightly but is still crumbly. Press into the bottom and 1-2 inches (3-5 cm) up the sides of the prepared springform pan. Bake the crust for 5 minutes, then cool on a cooling rack while preparing the filling.

② **Make the cheesecake filling.** In the bowl of a stand mixer, beat the soy cream cheese for about 1 minute until smooth and fluffy. Add the sugar and beat for 3 minutes, or until the sugar dissolves. Add the egg substitute, and beat until just combined, then add the sour cream and vanilla extract, beating well to incorporate. Pour the filling into the prepared crust.

③ **Bake.** Bake the cheesecake for 60-70 minutes, or until the top of the cheesecake is slightly golden. Remove the cake from the oven. Spread the soy sour cream over the surface to cover any cracks, and let the cheesecake cool on a wire cooling rack for 10-15 minutes. Run a sharp knife around the edges of the cake to loosen it from the sides, then cool the cake completely. Chill for 2 hours to overnight. Serve cold.

Chapter 13

JUST FOR KIDS

IF YOU PREPARE FOOD for children, you know that no subtleties escape them. Change up one of their favorite meals, and they will let you know just how much they notice. Children like to eat good food, too—meals that are fresh, savory, sweet, rich, and flavor abundant, and I've learned that, generally speaking, if the adults like the food, the kids will also. (The reverse does not always apply.)

I've also learned that kids eat healthily if healthy is the norm, but even kids who are transitioning from a more typical American diet will enjoy these dairy-free takes on the classics (and you will, too). Avocados and homemade Cashew Cheese make an Avocado Mac 'n Cheese (below) that will become a weekly staple, and your kids will never know that Homemade Fudge Pops (page 180), prepared with bananas and coconut cream, are good for them.

Avocado Mac n' Cheese

Infinitely healthier than the boxed stuff, this kid-friendly dish uses nutritious fats like avocados and nuts in place of dairy and adds tomatoes for color and texture.

YIELD: 4 SERVINGS

8 ounces (225 g) elbow pasta

3 large ripe avocados, peeled and pitted

1 tablespoon (15 mL) fresh lemon juice

1⅓ cups (315 mL) unsweetened almond milk

1 cup (260 g) grated Cashew Cheese (page 58), plus more for topping

1 tablespoon (8 g) nutritional yeast

¼ teaspoon sea salt, plus more to taste

½ cup (95 g) finely chopped tomatoes or halved grape tomatoes (optional)

(1) **Prepare the pasta.** Bring a pot of salted water to a boil and add the pasta. Cook until al dente, according to the manufacturer's instructions. Drain in a colander.

(2) **Make the cheese sauce.** Place the avocados, lemon juice, almond milk, grated Cashew Cheese, nutritional yeast, and sea salt in a blender. Blend until creamy. Return the pasta to the pot off the heat, and stir in the sauce. Fold in the tomatoes if using, and heat until warmed through. Serve immediately with sea salt to taste and a sprinkling of grated Cashew Cheese.

Cinnamon-Sugar Stars with Vanilla Almond Ice Cream

Here's a treat both you and the kids will enjoy. This recipe makes enough stars for about six servings, so feel free to make more or less according to your serving needs.

YIELD: 6 SERVINGS

FOR THE VANILLA ALMOND ICE CREAM:

Two 15-ounce (440 mL) cans coconut milk, refrigerated overnight

3 cups (705 mL) almond milk

1 cup (200 g) granulated sugar

¼ teaspoon sea salt

1 teaspoon vanilla extract

FOR THE CINNAMON STARS:

¼ cup (50 g) unrefined cane sugar

2 tablespoons (14 g) cinnamon

Four 10-inch (25 cm) flour tortillas, or more if desired

Canola or vegetable oil, for frying

① **Prepare the ice cream.** Puncture the cans of coconut milk and drain the liquid. Scoop out the coconut cream, and place 1 cup (235 mL) of the cream into a large bowl. (Save the remaining coconut cream for future use.) Add the almond milk, sugar, sea salt, and vanilla extract, and beat until the sugar is dissolved and the mixture is well combined. Chill for 1 hour. Place in the bowl of an ice cream maker, and freeze according to the manufacturer's instructions.

② **Make the cinnamon-sugar stars.** Combine the sugar and cinnamon in a small bowl. Using a pair of sharp scissors or a star-shaped cookie cutter, cut 3-inch stars out of the tortillas and set aside. Line a plate with paper towels. Fill a pot with about 2 inches (5 cm) of oil and heat until a deep-fry thermometer reads 350°F (180°C). Carefully place several stars in the hot oil, but don't crowd them. Cook for less than 1 minute, until puffed and golden brown (they will cook very quickly, so be ready!). Using a slotted spoon or spatula, remove the stars and transfer them to the paper towel–lined plate. Sprinkle with cinnamon-sugar mixture and repeat until you've fried all of the stars.

③ **Serve.** Place 2 scoops of the ice cream into bowls or cups, and place 2–3 stars in each serving. Serve immediately.

Cheesy Shells and Broccoli

A weeknight way to make broccoli fun, this simple dish is a winner with little palates.

YIELD: 4 SERVINGS

8 ounces (225 g) small shell pasta

2 cups (142 g) fresh broccoli florets

½ cup (60 g) nutritional yeast

¼ cup (47.5 g) finely ground cashews

3 tablespoons (24 g) all-purpose flour

½ teaspoon garlic powder

½ teaspoon onion powder

½ teaspoon sea salt, plus more to taste

2 cups (475 mL) unsweetened soymilk, almond milk, or hemp milk

2 tablespoons (30 mL) coconut oil

1 tablespoon (15 g) tahini

Freshly ground pepper

① **Prepare the pasta.** Bring a large pot of salted water to a rolling boil, and add the pasta. Cook until al dente, according to the manufacturer's instructions. When the pasta has 1 minute left, add the broccoli florets and cook for just 1 minute, or until the broccoli is bright green and tender-crisp. Drain the pasta and broccoli.

② **Make the sauce.** In the same pot off the heat, add the nutritional yeast, ground cashews, flour, garlic powder, onion powder, sea salt, and soymilk. Mix well and place over medium heat, stirring constantly to prevent burning. When the sauce has thickened slightly, add the coconut oil and tahini, stirring just to incorporate. Return the shells and broccoli to the pot, mixing just to combine. Serve immediately with sea salt and freshly ground pepper.

Falafel Pockets with Almond Yogurt Tzatziki

Baked falafel makes these traditionally fried treats a little healthier, and almond yogurt replaces the dairy in the sauce. Feel free to stuff these pockets with any veggies your child likes—you can even serve the falafel and tzatziki over rice.

YIELD: 4–6 SERVINGS

FOR THE ALMOND YOGURT TZATZIKI:

2 cups (460 g) plain unsweetened almond yogurt, store-bought or homemade (page 64)

1 cup (120 g) peeled and finely chopped cucumber, divided

1 teaspoon sea salt, plus more to taste

1 tablespoon (8 g) tapioca starch or cornstarch

1 tablespoon (15 mL) lemon juice

2 tablespoons (30 mL) extra-virgin olive oil

2 cloves garlic, minced

2 teaspoons (2 g) fresh dill

FOR THE FALAFEL:

Two 15-ounce (0.4 kg) cans chickpeas, drained and rinsed well

½ cup (25 g) finely chopped scallion, white and light green parts only

½ cup (55 g) finely grated fresh carrot

½ cup (30 g) finely chopped fresh parsley

2 cloves garlic

2 tablespoons (30 mL) olive oil

1 teaspoon cumin

¾ teaspoon baking powder

¼ cup (35 g) flour, or as needed

FOR ASSEMBLING:

Fresh baby spinach or lettuce

Chopped tomato

Sliced cucumber

Whole-wheat pitas

① **Prepare the tzatziki.** Place the almond yogurt, ½ cup (60 g) of the cucumber, sea salt, tapioca starch, lemon juice, olive oil, garlic, and dill in a blender. Blend until creamy. Stir in the remaining ½ cup (60 g) cucumber, transfer to a bowl, cover, and refrigerate for 1 hour to overnight.

② **Prepare the falafel.** Place the chickpeas, scallion, carrot, parsley, garlic, olive oil, and cumin in the bowl of a food processor. Process until combined but not pureed. Sprinkle the baking powder and then the flour over the top, and pulse several times to form a batter. If it sticks to your fingers, add more flour, 1 tablespoon (8 g) at a time, until the batter is still moist but not sticky. Transfer to a bowl and refrigerate for 2 hours to overnight.

③ **Bake.** Preheat the oven to 400°F (200°C, or gas mark 6). Lightly grease a large baking sheet with olive oil. Using a 2-ounce (55 g) portion scoop or your hands, shape the falafel mixture into balls the size of walnuts, and place on the prepared baking sheet. Bake for 10–15 minutes, or until golden brown.

④ **Assemble the pita pockets.** Insert the warm falafel, spinach or lettuce, tomatoes, and cucumbers into the pita breads. Place a dollop of the Almond Yogurt Tzatziki into each pocket and serve more on the side. Serve immediately.

Dairy-Free Pita Pizzas

Nothing beats a pita pizza when you don't have time to make the dough from scratch. This recipe uses a quick homemade pesto, a little bit of store-bought pizza sauce, grated dairy-free cheese, and veggies to make a quick but delicious dairy-free meal in under twenty minutes from start to finish.

YIELD: 4 SERVINGS

FOR THE BASIL PESTO:

1 cup (40 g) fresh basil leaves

½ cup (67 g) raw pine nuts

2 large cloves garlic

½ tablespoon (4 g) nutritional yeast

⅛ teaspoon sea salt, plus more to taste

2-4 tablespoons (30–60 mL) extra-virgin olive oil

FOR ASSEMBLY:

4 whole-wheat pitas

½ cup (90 g) pizza sauce, store-bought or homemade (page 129)

1 cup (260 g) grated dairy-free cheese, either store-bought or Cashew Cheese (page 58)

1 cup (150 g) chopped green bell pepper

1 cup (100 g) chopped pitted black olives

1. **Prepare the pan.** Preheat the oven to 450°F (230°C, or gas mark 8). Lightly oil a large baking sheet. Set aside.

2. **Make the pesto.** Place the basil, pine nuts, garlic, nutritional yeast, and sea salt in a blender. Process well, then add the olive oil while the machine is still running until the mixture just comes together into a paste.

3. **Assemble the pizzas.** Spread about 2 tablespoons (30 g) of the pesto onto each pita, followed by about 2 tablespoons (30 g) of pizza sauce. Top with the grated dairy-free cheese, then the bell pepper and black olives.

4. **Bake.** Bake for about 8–10 minutes, or until the pitas are lightly browned and the edges are crisp. Use a pizza cutter to slice the pizzas into quarters, and serve immediately.

Dairy-Free Scrambled Eggs with Ham

Prepared without milk or butter, scrambled eggs get a healthy boost in this simple recipe. Feel free to replace the ham with vegetarian meats, tofu, mushrooms, or vegetables if you prefer.

YIELD: 4 SERVINGS

6 large eggs

⅓ cup (80 mL) unsweetened soymilk or hemp milk

⅛ teaspoon sea salt, plus more to taste

¼ cup (25 g) chopped scallion, white and light green parts only

4 slices organic oven-roasted ham, ripped into pieces

Freshly ground black pepper

Cashew Cheese (page 58), optional

4 slices toast

1 **Prepare the eggs.** Whisk the eggs in a large bowl until beaten well. Add the soymilk and sea salt, beating well. Add the scallion and ham.

2 **Scramble.** Using a paper towel, lightly grease a frying pan with a little bit of margarine or coconut oil. Place over medium-high heat. Once the pan is hot, add the egg mixture, and let cook undisturbed for 1 minute. As the eggs begin to set, use a heat-resistant spatula to stir and scramble the eggs, tilting the pan occasionally to allow uncooked liquid parts to flow beneath cooked parts to prevent the eggs from browning. Once the eggs are lumpy and cooked through but not brown, they are done. Sprinkle with freshly ground pepper. Serve with the cheese, if desired, and immediately with toast.

Buckeye Bars

A tribute to the Ohio favorite, these peanut butter and chocolate treats are delightful for parties and potlucks, particularly when feeding kids. They're sweet and indulgent, and they're suitable for dairy-free, egg-free, gluten-free, and vegan diets.

YIELD: 32 BARS

FOR THE PEANUT BUTTER LAYER:

1 cup (224 g) nonhydrogenated soy margarine

4 cups (960 g) creamy natural peanut butter

8 cups (960 g) confectioners' sugar

2 tablespoons (16 g) tapioca starch

FOR THE CHOCOLATE LAYER:

16 ounces (455 g) good-quality dairy-free dark chocolate, chopped

Two 15-ounce (440 mL) cans coconut milk, refrigerated overnight

½ teaspoon vanilla extract

① **Prepare the peanut butter layer.** Line two 8-inch (20 cm) square baking pans with parchment paper, leaving about 1 inch (2.5 cm) overhang on all sides. In the bowl of a stand mixer, beat the soy margarine and peanut butter until smooth. Gradually add the confectioners' sugar and tapioca starch until the mixture is smooth. Spread into the prepared dishes, leveling the layer with an offset spatula. Chill for 2 hours.

② **Make the chocolate layer.** Place the chopped chocolate into a bowl just big enough to fit. Puncture the cans of coconut milk and drain out the liquid. Scoop out the coconut cream and add into a small saucepan along with the vanilla extract; place over medium-high heat. Heat until steam rises to the surface and bubbles form around the edges but the cream does not boil. Pour over the chopped chocolate, and allow to rest, undisturbed, for 5 minutes. Stir well until the chocolate is smooth and glossy.

③ **Assemble, chill, and serve.** Pour the chocolate layer over the peanut butter layer, and return to the refrigerator for 2–4 hours, or until set. When ready to serve, pull the bars out of the pans using the parchment paper and place on a cutting board. Using a sharp knife, slice into 2-inch (5 cm) squares. Serve cold.

Buttery Sugar Cookies

Shape these melt-in-your mouth cookies into any shapes that suit the occasion, and let the kids help cut them out, eating the dough as they go.

YIELD: ABOUT 4 DOZEN COOKIES

2½ cups (310 g) all-purpose flour

3 tablespoons (20 g) tapioca starch

1 teaspoon baking soda

1 teaspoon cream of tartar

½ cup (112 g) nonhydrogenated margarine, at room temperature

½ cup (120 mL) coconut oil, melted

1½ cups (180 g) confectioners' sugar

¼ cup (60 mL) unsweetened almond milk or soymilk, at room temperature

½ teaspoon vanilla extract

½ teaspoon almond extract

Unrefined cane sugar, for sprinkling

1) **Make the batter.** In a small bowl, mix together the flour, tapioca starch, baking soda, and cream of tartar. Set aside. In the bowl of a stand mixer, beat together the margarine and coconut oil. Gradually add the confectioners' sugar, almond milk, vanilla extract, and almond extract, beating just to combine. Add the dry ingredients and mix until a soft dough forms. Wrap tightly in plastic wrap and refrigerate for 15–20 minutes. Line a large baking sheet with parchment.

2) **Roll out the dough, cut the cookies, and chill.** Transfer the dough to a lightly floured surface, and roll out to about ¼ inch (6 mm) thick. Using lightly floured cookie cutters, cut into desired shapes and gently transfer to the parchment-lined baking sheet. Sprinkle lightly with unrefined cane sugar and return the sheet to the refrigerator for 1 hour. (This will keep the cookies from spreading while baking.)

3) **Bake.** Preheat the oven to 375°F (190°C, or gas mark 5). Take the cookie sheet out of the refridgerator and bake until golden, about 7–8 minutes. Cool for 10 minutes on the pan, then transfer to a wire cooling rack to cool completely.

Homemade Fudge Pops

By looking at the ingredients, it's hard to imagine that these pops taste like the real thing, but they do! Sweetened with bananas and maple syrup and made rich with coconut cream, these are a healthy version of the freezer-aisle favorite.

YIELD: 6–10 SERVINGS, DEPENDING ON POPSICLE SIZE

One 15-ounce (440 mL) can full-fat coconut milk, refrigerated overnight

3 large bananas

¼ cup (30 g) unsweetened cocoa powder

⅛ teaspoon sea salt

½ teaspoon vanilla extract

3 tablespoons (40 mL) pure maple syrup

1. **Prepare the coconut cream.** Puncture the can of coconut milk and drain out the liquid. Scoop the coconut cream into a blender.

2. **Blend, freeze, and enjoy.** Add the bananas, cocoa powder, sea salt, vanilla extract, and maple syrup and blend until thick and creamy. Pour into freezer pop molds and place in the freezer for 2–4 hours, or until frozen. Run the molds under warm water for 30 seconds when removing.

FIVE-MINUTE NO-DAIRY HOT CHOCOLATE

Rich, luscious, and perfect on cold winter days, this recipe takes just five minutes to prepare. Be sure to read your bittersweet chocolate label, as good-quality bittersweet chocolate is often dairy free, but lower-quality varieties sometimes include dairy ingredients such as milk solids.

YIELD: 4 SERVINGS

4 cups (940 mL) unsweetened almond milk, coconut milk, hemp milk, or soymilk

8 ounces (225 g) bittersweet chocolate, grated sugar, or other sweetener

Marshmallows or Coconut Milk Whipped Cream (page 168), for serving (optional)

Place the dairy-free milk and grated bittersweet chocolate in a small saucepan over medium-high heat. Bring to a boil, stirring constantly, and continue to boil for 1 minute. Remove from the heat, stirring constantly until all of the chocolate is melted. Add sugar to taste. Serve immediately, with marshmallows or Coconut Milk Whipped Cream, if desired.

Vanilla Ice Cream Sandwiches

Prepared with homemade Vanilla Bean Ice Cream (page 158) or store-bought, these treats are fun to make and eat. These bars are larger than traditional ones, so for smaller children, cut the bars in half to make 16 sandwiches.

YIELD: 8 SANDWICHES

FOR THE COOKIE LAYERS:

⅔ cup (160 mL) coconut milk

½ cup (100 g) unrefined cane sugar

⅓ cup (79 mL) canola oil

1 teaspoon cider vinegar

1 teaspoon vanilla extract

⅔ cup (80 g) all-purpose flour

⅓ cup (40 g) cocoa powder

½ teaspoon baking soda

¼ teaspoon baking powder

⅛ teaspoon salt

FOR THE ICE CREAM:

1 quart (0.9 L) Vanilla Bean Ice Cream (page 158) or store-bought dairy-free vanilla ice cream, softened

① **Make the cookie base.** Preheat the oven to 350°F (180°C, or gas mark 4). Lightly grease an 11 x 17-inch (28 x 43 cm) rimmed baking sheet, then line with parchment paper, leaving a slight overhang on the edges. In a large bowl, mix together the coconut milk, sugar, canola oil, vinegar, and vanilla extract. In another bowl, sift together the flour, cocoa powder, baking soda, baking powder, and salt until well mixed. Add the dry ingredients to the wet ingredients, and stir just until combined (do not overmix). Pour the batter onto the parchment-lined baking

sheet, leveling the cake base with a spatula if necessary. Bake for 7–10 minutes, or until the cake springs back when touched. Transfer to a wire cooling rack to cool completely.

② **Fill the cake.** Use the parchment paper to lift the cooled cake out of the baking sheet and transfer the cake to a cutting board. Cut the cake in half crosswise with a sharp knife. Place a piece of plastic wrap that's slightly larger than the cake on a clean work surface. Place one half of the cake top side down on the plastic wrap. Spread evenly with the softened ice cream. Carefully top the ice cream with the remaining half of the cake, top side up. (You can do this with your hands, or use the parchment paper to help you.) Transfer the cake back to the baking sheet, and wrap with plastic wrap. Place in the freezer for 2 hours to overnight.

③ **Cut into sandwiches.** Remove from the freezer and use a sharp knife to trim the edges all the way around to create straight edges on all sides, then cut into 8 rectangles. Poke the tops of the sandwiches with a fork in 3–4 places. Serve immediately.

Dairy-Free Resource Guide

Listed below are some of the companies and manufacturers whose products I regularly use in cooking and baking in my dairy-free kitchen. These products are available online and in stores, but I also recommend browsing through your farmers' markets and grocers for locally made dairy-free products.

Alter Eco Foods
A variety of organic, fair-trade products from rice and quinoa to sugar and decadent dark dairy-free chocolate
www.alterecofoods.com

Amande
This vegan, dairy-free, fruit juice–sweetened, gluten-free, soy-free almond milk yogurt that looks and tastes like the real thing is my favorite store-bought dairy-free yogurt substitute.
www.amandeyogurt.com

Bob's Red Mill
Producer of quality flours, grains, and baking mixes with gluten-free and dairy-free varieties; available at health food stores, online, and in organic sections of large grocers
www.bobsredmill.com

Daiya
The best dairy-free shredded cheese on the market, used in many restaurants; free of all "Top 8" allergens, GMO free, and widely available
www.daiyafoods.com

Earth Balance
A wide array of dairy-free products, including vegan, non-GMO, organic margarines produced from expeller-pressed oils; available in most groceries
www.earthbalancenatural.com

Eden Foods
A range of products for the dairy-free lifestyle, including non-GMO soy products and my preferred agar flakes
www.edenfoods.com

Enjoy Life Foods
Dairy-free products that are also free of all "Top 8" allergens and prepared in a dedicated nut-free facility
www.enjoylifefoods.com

EuroCuisine Automatic Yogurt Maker YM100
A relatively inexpensive yogurt maker that makes professional-grade yogurt at home; available online and in specialty cookware stores
www.eurocuisine.net

Nasoya
Organic, non-GMO tofu products
www.nasoya.com

Nutiva Organics
Purveyors of high-quality organic coconut oil and hemp oil; available in many groceries and online
www.nutiva.com

So Delicious
Widely distributed dairy-free ice creams, almond milk beverages, soymilk beverages, coconut milk beverages, dairy-free creamers, and dairy-free yogurts; non-GMO
www.sodeliciousdairyfree.com

Spectrum Organics
High-quality expeller-pressed cooking oils, including organic canola oil, coconut oil, flax oil, and olive oil; Spectrum also makes some of the most delicious vegan and non-vegan mayonnaise I've ever tried
www.spectrumorganics.com

Sunspire
Dairy-free, vegan, and other alternative chocolate products, including dairy-free semisweet chocolate chips and vegan carob chips
www.sunspire.com

Thai Kitchen
The best organic canned coconut milk on the market; widely distributed
www.thaikitchen.com

Vitamix
Manufacturer of professional-grade blenders useful in many aspects of dairy-free cookery, including grinding nuts and pureeing soups
www.vitamix.com

Wholesome Sweeteners
Producer of organic, fair trade sweeteners and unrefined sugars produced without bleaching agents; every recipe that calls for unrefined cane sugar in this book was made with this company's Fair Trade Certified Organic Sugar
www.wholesomesweeteners.com

References

CHAPTER 1

Åkerblom, Hans K., and Mikael Knip. "Putative Environmental Factors in Type 1 Diabetes." *Diabetes / Metabolism Reviews* 14.1 (1998): 31–68.

Campbell, T. Colin, and Thomas M. Campbell. *The China Study: The Most Comprehensive Study of Nutrition Ever Conducted and the Startling Implications for Diet, Weight Loss and Long-Term Health.* Dallas, TX: BenBella, 2005.

Chan, J. M., and E. L. Giovannucci. "Dairy Products, Calcium, and Vitamin D and Risk of Prostate Cancer." *Epidemiological Reviews* 23.1 (2001): 87–92.

Esselstyn, Caldwell B. "Resolving the Coronary Artery Disease Epidemic through Plant-Based Nutrition." *Preventive Cardiology* 4.4 (2001): 171–77.

Feskanich, D., et al. "Milk, Dietary Calcium, and Bone Fractures in Women: A 12-year Prospective Study." *American Journal of Public Health* 87.6 (1997): 992–97.

Frassetto, L. A., et al. "Worldwide Incidence of Hip Fracture in Elderly Women: Relation to Consumption of Animal and Vegetable Foods." *Journals of Gerontology* 55.10 (2000): 585–92.

Gupta, Ruchi S., et al. "The Prevalence, Severity, and Distribution of Childhood Food Allergy in the United States." *Pediatrics* 128.1 (2011).

"Health Concerns about Dairy Products." *Physician Committee for Responsible Medicine*, 2012. www.pcrm.org/health/diets/vegdiets/health-concerns-about-dairy-products.

Jacobson, Hilary. *Mother Food: For Breastfeeding Mothers: Foods and Herbs That Promote Milk Production and a Mother's Health.* [S.n.]: Mother Food Series, 2004. 138–40.

Karjalainen, Jukka, et al. "A Bovine Albumin Peptide as a Possible Trigger of Insulin-Dependent Diabetes Mellitus." *New England Journal of Medicine* 327.5 (1992): 302–7.

Kradijan, Robert. "The Milk Letter: A Message to My Patients." *New York Times Magazine*, October 6, 2002.

Law, M. R., and N. J. Wald. "An Ecological Study of Serum Cholesterol and Ischaemic Heart Disease between 1950 and 1990." *European Journal of Clinical Nutrition* 48.5 (1994): 305–25.

McBean, L., and G. Miller. "Allaying Fears and Fallacies about Lactose Intolerance." *Journal of the American Dietetic Association* 98.6 (1998): 671–76.

Naik, R. G., and J. P. Palmer. "Preservation of Beta-cell Function in Type 1 Diabetes." *Diabetes Reviews* 7 (1999): 154–82.

Pickarski, Ron. "The Protein Issue and Vegetarianism. (High-Protein Diets May Increase Chances of Osteoporosis; Includes Vegetarian Recipes)." *Total Health.* Total Health Communications, Inc., 1990.

Sicherer, Scott. "Clinical Implications of Cross-reactive Food Allergens." *Journal of Allergy and Clinical Immunology* 108.6 (2001): 881–90.

Woodford, K. B. *Devil in the Milk: Illness, Health and Politics of A1 and A2 Milk.* White River Junction, VT: Chelsea Green Pub., 2007.

CHAPTER 2

Balch, James F., and Phyllis A. Balch. "Calcium." *Prescription for Nutritional Healing.* 2nd ed. Garden City Park, NY: Avery Pub. Group, 1997. 23–24.

Brown, Amy C. *Understanding Food: Principles and Preparation.* Belmont, CA: Thomson/Wadsworth, 2008.

"Calcium." Calcium QuickFacts. Office of Dietary Supplements National Institutes of Health, March 14, 2013. http://ods.od.nih.gov/factsheets/Calcium-QuickFacts.

Michel, Beat A., Daniel A. Bloch, and James F. Fries. "Weight-Bearing Exercise, Overexercise, and Lumbar Bone Density Over Age 50 Years." *Archives of Internal Medicine* 149.10 (1989): 2325–29.

"Vitamin D Health Professional Fact Sheet." *Office of Dietary Supplements,* National Institutes of Health, June 24, 2011. Web. http://ods.od.nih.gov/factsheets/VitaminD-Health-Professional.

CHAPTER 3

Adebamowo, C., et al. "High School Dietary Dairy Intake and Teenage Acne." *Journal of the American Academy of Dermatology* 52.2 (2005): 207–14.

Baker, Mitzi. "Vitamin E and Cancer Risk." *Cancer Today* 2.4 (2012). www.cancertodaymag.org/Winter2012/Pages/vitamin-e-and-cancer-risk-.aspx.

Balch, James F., and Phyllis A. Balch. "Magnesium" and "Phosphorous." *Prescription for Nutritional Healing.* Garden City Park, NY: Avery Pub. Group, 1997. 26–28.

Balch, James F., and Phyllis A. Balch. "Vitamin E." *Prescription for Nutritional Healing.* 2nd ed. Garden City Park, NY: Avery Pub. Group, 1997. 19–20.

Cohen, Ashley E., and Carol S. Johnston. "Almond Ingestion at Mealtime Reduces Postprandial Glycemia and Chronic Ingestion Reduces Hemoglobin A1c in Individuals with Well-controlled Type 2 Diabetes Mellitus." *Metabolism* 60.9 (2011): 1312–17.

Davis, P., and C. Iwahashi. "Whole Almonds and Almond Fractions Reduce Aberrant Crypt Foci in a Rat Model of Colon Carcinogenesis." *Cancer Letters* 165.1 (2001): 27–33.

Greenwald, P., E. Lanza, and G. A. Eddy. "Dietary Fiber in the Reduction of Colon Cancer Risk." *Journal of the American Dietetic Association* 87.9 (1987): 1178–88.

Jenkins, D. J., et al. "Almonds Decrease Postprandial Glycemia, Insulinemia, and Oxidative Damage in Healthy Individuals." *Journal of Nutrition* 136 (2006): 2987–92.

Jenkins, D. J., et al. "Dose Response of Almonds on Coronary Heart Disease Risk Factors: Blood Lipids, Oxidized Low-Density Lipoproteins, Lipoprotein(a), Homocysteine, and Pulmonary Nitric Oxide: A Randomized, Controlled, Crossover Trial." *Circulation* 106 (2002): 1327–32.

Josse, A., et al. "Almonds and Postprandial Glycemia—A Dose-Response Study." *Metabolism* 56.3 (2007): 400–4.

Klein, E. A., et al. "Vitamin E and the Risk of Prostate Cancer: The Selenium and Vitamin E Cancer Prevention Trial (SELECT)." *The Journal of the American Medical Association* 306.14 (2011): 1549–56.

Kris-Etherton, Penny M., et al. "The Effects of Nuts on Coronary Heart Disease Risk." *Nutrition Reviews* 59.4 (2001): 103–11.

Liao, Fangzi, Aaron R. Folsom, and Frederick L. Brancati. "Is Low Magnesium Concentration a Risk Factor for Coronary Heart Disease? The Atherosclerosis Risk in Communities (ARIC) Study." *American Heart Journal* 136.3 (1998): 480–90.

"Magnesium: A Health Professional Fact Sheet." Office of Dietary Supplements, National Institutes of Health, July 13, 2009. http://ods.od.nih.gov/factsheets/Magnesium-HealthProfessional

Ohlsson, Lena. "Dairy Products and Plasma Cholesterol Levels." *Food & Nutrition Research* 54.0 (2010).

Preedy, Victor R., Ronald R. Watson, and Vinood B. Patel. "Almonds (*Prunus Dulcis*): Post-Ingestive Hormonal Response." In *Nuts & Seeds in Health and Disease Prevention.* London: Academic, 2011.

Rude, R. K., and M. Olerich. "Magnesium Deficiency: Possible Role in Osteoporosis Associated with Gluten-sensitive Enteropathy." *Osteoporosis International* 6.6 (1996): 453–61.

Scott, Jess C. *Clear: A Guide to Treating Acne Naturally.* JessINK, 2012.

"The SELECT Prostate Cancer Prevention Trial." *National Cancer Institute.* October 12, 2011. www.cancer.gov/clinicaltrials/noteworthy-trials/select/Page1.

Spiller, G. A., et al. "Effect of a Diet High in Monounsaturated Fat from Almonds on Plasma Cholesterol and Lipoproteins." *Journal of the American College of Nutrition* 11.2 (1992): 126–30.

Stein, Rob. "Study: More Milk Means More Weight Gain." *The Washington Post,* June 7, 2005.

"Tree Nut Allergies." Food Allergy Research & Education. Web. www.foodallergy.org/allergens/tree-nut-allergy.

Wien, D., et al. "Almond Consumption and Cardiovascular Risk Factors in Adults with Prediabetes." *Journal of the American College of Nutrition* 29.3 (2010): 189–97.

Wien, M. A., et al. "Almonds vs Complex Carbohydrates in a Weight Reduction Program." *International Journal of Obesity* 27.11 (2003): 1365–72.

CHAPTER 4

Anderson, J. W., B. M. Johnstone, and M. E. Cook-Newell. "Meta-analysis of the Effects of Soy Protein Intake on Serum Lipids." *New England Journal of Medicine* 333.5 (1995): 276–82.

Barnard, Neal. "Soy and Your Health." Huffingtonpost.com. August 23, 2012. www.huffingtonpost.com/neal-barnard-md/soy-health_b_1822291.html.

Bowden, Jonny. "Soy Foods." In *The 150 Healthiest Foods on Earth: The Surprising, Unbiased Truth about What You Should Eat and Why.* Gloucester, MA: Fair Winds, 2007. 166–67.

"Breast Cancer Prevention." *National Cancer Institute.* www.cancer.gov/cancertopics/pdq/prevention/breast/Patient.

DesMaisons, Kathleen. "Sorting Out the Soy Story." Radiant Recovery, 2003. http://radiantrecovery.com/soy4303html.htm.

Dona, Artemis, and Ioannis Arvanitoyannis. "Health Risks of Genetically Modified Foods." *Critical Reviews in Food Science and Nutrition* 49.2 (2009): 164–75.

Fernandez-Cornejo, Jorge. "Adoption of Genetically Engineered Crops in the U.S.: Recent Trends in GE Adoption." USDA, July 5, 2012. www.ers.usda.gov/data-products/adoption-of-genetically-engineered-crops-in-the-us/recent-trends-in-ge-adoption.aspx.

Gardner, Christopher D., et al. "Effect of Two Types of Soy Milk and Dairy Milk on Plasma Lipids in Hypercholesterol-emic Adults: A Randomized Trial." *Journal of the American College of Nutrition* 26.6 (2006): 669–77.

"Information about Asthma, Allergies, Food Allergies and More!" Asthma and Allergy Foundation of America, 2005. www.aafa.org/display.cfm?id=9.

James, Clive. Brief 44: *Global Status of Commercialized Biotech/GM Crops: 2012*. Ithaca, NY: ISAAA, 2012.

Nestle, Marion. "Soy Milk: Panacea, or Just Another Food." In *What to Eat*. New York: North Point, 2007. 128–37.

O'Connor, Anahad. "Really? The Claim: Eating Soy Increases the Risk of Breast Cancer." *The New York Times* June 26, 2012, New York ed., D5.

Shu, X. O., et al. "Soy Food Intake and Breast Cancer Survival." *Journal of the American Medical Association* 302.22 (2009): 2437–443.

Spiroux De Vendômois, Joël, et al. "Debate on GMOs Health Risks after Statistical Findings in Regulatory Tests." *International Journal of Biological Sciences* 6.6 (2010): 590–98.

Willett, Walter, et al. "The Scoop on Soy." In *Eat, Drink, and Be Healthy: The Harvard Medical School Guide to Healthy Eating*. New York: Simon & Schuster, 2005. 127–28.

Wu, A. H., et al. "Epidemiology of Soy Exposures and Breast Cancer Risk." *British Journal of Cancer* 98.1 (2008): 9–14.

CHAPTER 5

Clark, Melissa. "Once a Villain, Coconut Oil Charms the Health Food World." *The New York Times,* March 2, 2011, New York ed., sec. D;1.

Enig, Mary G. "Coconut: In Support of Good Health in the 21st Century." Lecture, Asian Pacific Coconut Community 30th Anniversary. www.hgm.com.my/images/download/ENIG.pdf.

Fife, Bruce. "Coconut Oil and Medium-Chain Triglycerides." Coconut Research Center, 2003. www.coconutresearchcenter.org/article10612.htm.

Isaacs, Charles E., Richard E. Litov, and Halldor Thormar. "Antimicrobial Activity of Lipids Added to Human Milk, Infant Formula, and Bovine Milk." *The Journal of Nutritional Biochemistry* 6.7 (1995): 362–66.

Nevin, K., and T. Rajamohan. "Beneficial Effects of Virgin Coconut Oil on Lipid Parameters and in Vitro LDL Oxidation." *Clinical Biochemistry* 37.9 (2004): 830–35.

Preuss, Harry G., et al. "Minimum Inhibitory Concentrations of Herbal Essential Oils and Monolaurin for Gram-positive and Gram-negative Bacteria." *Molecular and Cellular Biochemistry* 272.1-2 (2005): 29–34.

"Shining the Spotlight on Trans Fats." *The Nutrition Source.* Harvard School of Public Health. www.hsph.harvard.edu/nutritionsource/transfats

Thormar, H., et al. "Hydrogels Containing Monocaprin Have Potent Microbicidal Activities against Sexually Transmitted Viruses and Bacteria in Vitro." *Sexually Transmitted Infections* 75.3 (1999): 181–85.

Thormar, H., H. Hilmarsson, and G. Bergsson. "Stable Concentrated Emulsions of the 1-Monoglyceride of Capric Acid (Monocaprin) with Microbicidal Activities against the Food-Borne Bacteria *Campylobacter jejuni, Salmonella spp.,* and *Escherichia coli*." *Applied and Environmental Microbiology* 72.1 (2006): 522–6.

CHAPTER 6

"Arsenic in Your Food." *Consumer Reports,* November 2012. Web. www.consumerreports.org/cro/magazine/2012/11/arsenic-in-your-food/index.htm.

"Brown Rice and Cardiovascular Protection." *American Physiological Society*, October 13, 2009. www.the-aps.org/mm/hp/Audiences/Public-Press/For-the-Press/releases/10/13.html.

Ginsberg, Gary. "What's the Advice for Arsenic in Rice?" TheHuffingtonPost.com, December 11, 2012. www.huffingtonpost.com/dr-gary-ginsberg/whats-the-advice-for-arse_b_2218448.html.

Hu, Emily A., et al. "White Rice Consumption and Risk of Type 2 Diabetes: Meta-analysis and Systematic Review." *British Medical Journal* 344 (2012).

Jonnalagadda, Satya S., et al. "Putting the Whole Grain Puzzle Together: Health Benefits Associated with Whole Grains—Summary of American Society for Nutrition 2010 Satellite Symposium." *Journal of Nutrition* 141.5 (2011): 10,115–225.

Mann, Denise. "White Bread, Rice, and Other Carbs Boost Heart Disease Risk in Women." CNN.com, April 12, 2010. www.cnn.com/2010/HEALTH/04/12/glycemic.diet.heart/index.html.

Milner, J. A. "Functional Foods and Health Promotion." *The Journal of Nutrition* 129.7 (1999): 1395–97.

Most, Marlene M., et al. "Rice Bran Oil, Not Fiber, Lowers Cholesterol in Humans." *The American Journal of Clinical Nutrition* 81.1 (2005): 64–68.

Pereira, M. A., et al. "Dietary Fiber and Risk of Coronary Heart Disease: A Pooled Analysis of Cohort Studies." *Archives of Internal Medicine* 164.4 (2004): 370–76.

Schattner, Elaine. "So There's Arsenic in Our Rice—Now What?" *The Atlantic* (2012).

Sheaffer, Virginia, and Giselle Zayon. "Temple Study Points to Cardiovascular Benefits of Brown Rice." Temple University School of Medicine, May 5, 2010. www.temple.edu/medicine/eguchi_brown_rice.htm.

Sun, Q., D., et al. "White Rice, Brown Rice, and Risk of Type 2 Diabetes in US Men and Women." *Archives of Internal Medicine* 170.11 (2010): 961–69.

"USA Rice Federation Statement on Arsenic in Rice." *USA Rice Federation*, December 6, 2012. www.usarice.com/index.php?option=com_content&view=article&id=1686:usa-rice-federation-statement-on-arsenic-in-rice&catid=84:usarice-newsroom&Itemid=327.

Wolk, Alicja, et al. "Long-term Intake of Dietary Fiber and Decreased Risk of Coronary Heart Disease Among Women." *Journal of the American Medical Association* 281.21 (1999): 1998–2004.

CHAPTER 7

Bowden, Jonny. "Hemp Seed Oil." In *The 150 Healthiest Foods on Earth: The Surprising, Unbiased Truth about What You Should Eat and Why.* Gloucester, MA: Fair Winds, 2007. 306–7.

Chang, C. S., et al. "Gamma-linolenic Acid Inhibits Inflammatory Responses by Regulating NF-kappaB and AP-1 Activation in Lipopolysaccharide-induced RAW 264.7 Macrophages." *Inflammation* 33.1 (2010): 46–57.

Connor, William E. "Importance of N-3 Fatty Acids in Health and Disease." *The American Journal of Clinical Nutrition* 71.1 (2000): 171S–175S.

Erasmus, Udo. *Fats That Heal, Fats That Kill: The Complete Guide to Fats, Oils, Cholesterol, and Human Health.* Burnaby, BC, Canada: Alive, 1993. 288–91.

Harris, W. S., et al. "Omega-6 Fatty Acids and Risk for Cardiovascular Disease: A Science Advisory from the American Heart Association Nutrition Subcommittee of the Council on Nutrition, Physical Activity, and Metabolism; Council on Cardiovascular Nursing; and Council on Epidemiology and Prevention." *Circulation* 119.6 (2009): 902–7.

Lando, Laura. "The New Science Behind America's Deadliest Diseases." *The Wall Street Journal.* July 16, 2012. http://online.wsj.com/article/SB10001424052702303612804577531092453590070.html.

Preedy, Victor R., Ronald R. Watson, and Vinood B. Patel. "Chapter 74: Medicinal Use of Hempseeds (*Cannabis Sativa L.*): Effects on Platelet Aggregation." In *Nuts & Seeds in Health and Disease Prevention.* London: Academic, 2011. 640–43.

Rodriguez-Leyva, Delfin, and Grant N. Pierce. "The Cardiac and Haemostatic Effects of Dietary Hempseed." *Nutrition & Metabolism* 7.1 (2010): 32.

Schwab, U. S., et al. "Effects of Hempseed and Flaxseed Oils on the Profile of Serum Lipids, Serum Total and Lipoprotein Lipid Concentrations and Haemostatic Factors." *European Journal of Nutrition* 45.8 (2006): 470–77.

Simopoulos, Artemis P., Alexander Leaf, and Norman Salem, Jr. "Workshop on the Essentiality of and Recommended Dietary Intakes for Omega-6 and Omega-3 Fatty Acids." *Journal of the American College of Nutrition* 18.5 (1999): 487–89.

Acknowledgments

This book, like most aspects of cooking, is a collaborative work. I am grateful to so many people for its progression from idea to reality. First, I am grateful to my husband, Brian—your partnership in all areas of my life has enriched everything I do and see in this world. To my son, Elliott: I had no idea such a small person could inspire me in such a big way. To Beth, my sister: thank you for eating my food for so many years, and for always dreaming big with me. To my aunt, uncle, and cousins for allowing me to experiment in your kitchen in those early years, and for always pushing me forward. To my mom, for encouraging me to read everything I could get my hands on. To my dad, for telling me that I could do anything.

A huge thanks to everyone at Fair Winds Press and to my agent, Marilyn Allen, is in order. I am so very grateful to Jill Alexander and Dianne Jacob for polishing my words into something that resembles a book, and to Marilyn for setting this faraway idea into motion.

Thanks to the About.com team for all that you do and have done to keep Dairyfreecooking.about.com up and running for the past six years. I am proud to be a contributor to your vast network of information.

Thanks to every publication that has published and continues to publish my work, including the *Alaska Dispatch, Anchorage Daily News, Anchorage Press, GOOD, Narrative, San Francisco Medicine,* and *Tundra Telegraph.*

Last but not least, thanks to all of the readers who have offered feedback and contributed to our community of mindful, healthy eating and living. Your e-mails, recipe comments, and words of support have been invaluable.

About the Author

Ashley Adams has worked in many fields of the dairy-free food industry, including teaching vegan cooking classes, creating vegan and dairy-free recipes for restaurants, and writing about dairy-free cooking at Dairyfreecooking.about.com. More than 1,000 of her personal recipes are available online. She currently works as a full-time freelance writer and writes for various publications about food, health, and well-being. She lives, cooks, photographs, and writes in Anchorage, Alaska, with her husband, Brian, and son, Elliott.agar, 14

Index